AN INTRODUCTION TO

PAINTING IN OILS

AN INTRODUCTION TO

PAINTING IN OILS

HAZEL HARRISON

**Eagle
Editions**

A QUANTUM BOOK

Published by Eagle Editions Ltd
11 Heathfield
Royston
Hertfordshire SG8 5BW

Copyright ©MCMLXXXVII
Quintet Publishing Ltd

This edition printed 2000

ISBN 1-86160-365-7

QUMIPO

This book is produced by
Quantum Publishing
6 Blundell Street
London N7 9BH

Printed in Singapore by
Star Standard Industries Pte Ltd

CONTENTS

CHAPTER ONE
WHY OILS?

IN recent decades there has been an amazing pro-
liferation of new materials for artists and de-
signers, so much so that a visit to one of the larger
artists' suppliers can leave an uninitiated person feeling confused and bewildered. There are pencils, pens,
crayons and pastels in every colour of the rainbow;
there are acrylic paints, both in tubes and in pots;
there are watercolours in tubes, pans and boxes; there
are gouaches and poster paints; there are even special
paints for fabrics and ceramics. Indeed, special
materials are now available for almost any surface
that could conceivably be painted or decorated. And,
often tucked away unobtrusively in one corner, there
are oil paints.

Why, then, are oil paints still so popular with professional artists and 'Sunday painters' alike? There are
two main reasons for this, the first being that oil paint
is the most versatile of all the painting media, and can
be used in any number of ways to suit all styles, subjects and sizes of work. The second is that it is the
easiest medium for a beginner to use. Which is not to
say, of course, that a novice will automatically be able
to create a masterpiece at first try – that is most unlikely. But because oil paint can be manipulated,
scraped off and overpainted, built up and then
scraped down once again, it enables you to learn by
trial and error, uninhibited by the thought of having
'to start all over again', or waste expensive materials.
This is not true of any other medium: acrylic, for
example, cannot be moved at all once it has been laid
down, and watercolour – a lovely medium but a tricky
once – quickly loses all its qualities of freshness and
translucence if overworked. Of course, an overworked
oil painting will not be a perfect picture, but it may at
least be a creditable one, if only because of the knowledge gained in painting it.

OIL PAINT IN THE PAST

Oil paint, though regarded as a 'traditional' painting
medium, is actually quite young in terms of art history.
In Europe, before the invention of oil paint in the
15th century, artists painted with tempera, which is
colour pigment bound with egg yolk. This was a difficult medium to use as it dried very fast, and thus
called for a deliberate and meticulous approach.

The Flemish painter Jan van Eyck (c.1390-1441)
was the first to experiment with raw pigments bound
with an oil mixture, when he found that one of his
tempera paintings had split while drying in the sun.
Not only did the oil paints dry without cracking, but,
as van Eyck discovered, they could be applied in thin,
transparent layers which gave the colours a depth and
luminosity hitherto unknown.

The early painters in oil, like van Eyck, used the
paint thinly, with delicate brushstrokes that are
almost invisible to the eye. But the full potential of oil
paint was not really exploited until it was taken up by
the Italian painters of the 15th and 16th centuries,

LEFT *Self Portrait* by Rembrandt van Rijn (1606-69). Rembrandt shocked many of his contemporaries by his bold use of paint, which produced thick, textured surfaces. The popular Dutch paintings of the time were characterized by a very smooth finish, with no visible brushstrokes, while in Rembrandt's later work brushstrokes and the paint itself are used to suggest texture, the paint being used almost as a modelling medium in places.

LEFT *Old Woman with a Rosary* by Paul Cézanne (1839-1906). By Cézanne's time, the techniques of oil painting had been largely freed from the earlier restrictions and prejudices. The brushstrokes are an integral part of this dramatic composition, as are the areas of broken colour, while the face itself has been treated in a bold, broad manner as a series of planes.

RIGHT *Man in a Turban* by Jan van Eyck (active 1422-41). In his oil paintings, van Eyck used much the same methods as previously used for tempera work, building up thin layers of paint, one over another, the technique known as glazing. However, oil paint used in this way gives a depth and luminosity of effect which cannot be achieved with tempera.

notably Giorgione (1475-1510) and Titian (*c*.1487-1576).

In Titian's hands, and later in those of the great Dutch painter Rembrandt (1606-69), oil paint was at last used with a feeling for its own inherent qualities. Both artists combined delicately painted areas of glazing (thin paint applied in layers over one another) with thick brushstrokes in which the actual marks of the brush became a feature rather than something to be disguised. Rembrandt's later paintings must have seemed quite shocking to a public accustomed to the smooth, satin finish of other contemporary Dutch paintings – a common complaint was that they looked unfinished.

The English landscape painter John Constable (1776-1837), and the French Impressionists later in the 19th century, took the freedom of painting to even greater lengths by using oil as a quick sketching medium, often working out of doors. In Constable's day the camera had yet to be invented, and artists had of necessity to make a great many sketches as references for their finished works. Constable's wonderful sky and landscape studies, made rapidly, often on scraps of paper and cardboard, were never intended as finished works of art; but to our eyes they are much more pleasing, and infinitely more exciting, than his large polished studio paintings, because they have the quality of immediacy that landscape painting seems to demand.

The Impressionists, who drew inspiration from Constable, applied their paint in thick dabs and strokes of broken colour to depict what was their main preoccupation – the ever-changing effects of light on the landscape. Vincent van Gogh (1853-90), who was not an Impressionist but is sometimes grouped with them because he was working at much the same time, used both the colour and the texture of the paint to express his emotions and to define forms, treating the paint almost as a modelling medium. We are so familiar with van Gogh's paintings through countless reproductions that it is hard to appreciate how strange, indeed even offensive, those great, thick, swirling brushstrokes must have looked to his contemporaries (van Gogh sold only one painting during his entire lifetime).

OIL PAINT TODAY

The very diversity of painting techniques in the past has had the effect of freeing us from any preconceptions about the medium. It is what you want it to be; there is no 'right' or 'wrong' way of doing an oil painting. Today's painters use oil paint in so many different ways that it is often hard to believe that the same medium has been used. Interestingly, the art of tempera painting is now undergoing a revival, and some artists working in oil use a similar technique, applying thin layers of transparent glazes to produce a luminous, light-filled quality. Other artists apply paint thickly with a knife, building it up on the surface of the canvas so that it resembles a relief sculpture.

New painting mediums – oils, varnishes and extenders – are constantly being developed in recognition of these different needs; for example, you can choose one type of medium if you want to build up delicate glazes, another if you want to achieve a thick, textured surface using the impasto technique.

Oil paints can be mixed with other types of paint and even other media; for instance, they can be used in conjunction with oil pastels for quick and dramatic effects; they can be drawn into with pencils; and some artists even mix paint with sand to create areas of texture. A later chapter treats such special techniques in more detail, but the foregoing should give you some idea of the creative potential of this exciting and adaptable medium.

OPPOSITE TOP LEFT *Autumn at Argenteuil* by Claude Monet (1840-1926). The French Impressionists were very much influenced by Constable's landscape paintings, and Monet in particular took the preoccupation with the effects of light almost to the point of an obsession. He frequently worked out of doors, and would paint several versions of the same scene in different lights, building up the paint in thick impastos to achieve the ever-changing effects suggestive of motion which he sought.

FAR LEFT *Olive Trees* by Vincent van Gogh (1853-90). The Impressionists' use of paint was free and daring by the academic standards of the day, but van Gogh's was the most innovative by far, and even those accustomed to the newer styles found his paintings perplexing and even shocking. No one had hitherto dared to represent the sky or foliage as a series of thickly-painted swirls, as in this painting, or the ground as broken lines of bright, unblended colour.

LEFT *Chain Pier, Brighton* by John Constable (1776-1837). Constable was among the first artists to use oil paint as a sketching medium, and his small studies, often on pieces of paper or primed cardboard, are infinitely fresher and more spontaneous than his large studio canvases. This tiny sketch, no more than 25 cm (10 in) high, makes a complete statement about light and colour, as well as recording all the important details of the scene.

11

CHAPTER TWO

MATERIALS AND EQUIPMENT

MATERIALS for oil painting can be costly; so it is advisable to work out your 'starter kit' carefully. Begin by buying the minimum and adding extra colours, brushes and so on when you have progressed to the stage of understanding your particular requirements. For example, someone who intends to specialize in flower painting will need a different range of colours from someone whose chosen theme is seascapes, while a person working on a miniature scale will use brushes quite unlike those needed for large-scale paintings.

CHOOSING PAINTS

Oil paints are divided into two main categories: artists' and students' colours. The latter are cheaper because they contain less pure pigment and more fillers and extenders, but in general they are a false economy for that very reason; they cannot provide the same intensity of colour as the more expensive range. However, students' colours are fine for practising with, and it is possible to combine the two types using the students' colours for browns and other colours where intensity is not a prime requirement and artists' for the pure colours such as red, yellow and blue. A large-size tube of white works out most economical, since white is used more than most other colours.

Paints in the artists' range are not all the same price – a trap for the unwary. They are classified in series, usually from 1 to 7 (different manufacturers have different methods of classification), series 7 being extremely expensive. The price differences reflect the expense and/or scarcity of the pigment used. Nowadays, because there are so many excellent chemical pigments, it is seldom necessary to use the very expensive colours, such as vermilion, except in very special cases.

It is often said that all colours can be mixed from the three primaries, red, yellow and blue. To some extent this is true, but they will certainly not provide a subtle or exciting range, and in any case there are a great many different versions of red, yellow and blue. The illustration shows a suggested 'starter palette', which should provide an adequate mix of colours for most purposes. In general you will need, as well as white, a warm and a cool version of each of the primaries, plus a brown and a green and perhaps a violet or purple. Strictly speaking, greens are not essential as they can be mixed from blue and yellow, but it takes time and experience to arrive at the right hue, and there really is not much point in spending more time in mixing than you need. Vividian is a good choice, since it mixes well with any colour. Other useful additions to your palette are rose madder in the red group; a lemon yellow such as Winsor or cadmium lemon in the yellow group; cerulean blue and Antwerp or cobalt blue in the blue group; and sap green and chrome green in the greens. Good browns and greys are burnt sienna, burnt umber and Payne's grey. Flake white dries

ABOVE A suggested 'starter palette'. From right to left: white (above), yellow ochre, cadmium yellow, cadmium red, alizarin crimson, cobalt violet, ultramarine, Prussian blue and viridian.

The palette chosen depends very much on the subject to be painted: for

instance, violet might not be needed at all, cobalt blue might be used instead of the other two blues, an additional green, such as chrome oxide, added, and a different yellow chosen.

The photograph shows the colours mixed with varying amounts of white.

quickly and is resistant to cracking, but it contains poisonous lead; for this reason some artists prefer to use titanium white, which is non-toxic. The use of black is often frowned upon, and many artists never use it as it can have a deadening effect, but it can be mixed with yellow to produce a rich olive green, and many landscape artists use it for this purpose.

PAINTING MEDIUMS

Oil paint can be used just as it comes from the tube, or it can be a combination of oil and a thinner (what artists call a *medium*). If you try to apply undiluted paint accurately in a small area, you will see why such mediums are necessary; without them the paint is not easily malleable.

The most popular medium is the traditional blend of linseed oil and turpentine or white spirit, usually in a ratio of 60% oil and 40% thinner. Linseed oil dries to a glossy finish which is resistant to cracking – but be sure to buy either purified or cold-pressed linseed oil, which dry without yellowing. Boiled linseed oil – the sort found in DIY shops – contains impurities which cause rapid yellowing.

Linseed oil is slow to dry, which may not suit your way of working and can produce a rather churned-up paint surface. There are several faster-drying mediums available, such as drying linseed oil, drying poppy oil, stand oil (which also makes the paint flow well and disguises brushstrokes) and an alkyd-based medium sold under the name of *Liquin*.

Turpentine is the most commonly used artist's thinner, though in fact white spirit is just as good and is less likely to cause the headaches and allergic reactions which artists sometimes complain of when using turpentine. White spirit also has less odour, and stores without deteriorating.

Special ready-mixed painting mediums are sold for specific purposes. Linseed oil, for instance, is not suitable for glazing (see p. 27) as it will dribble down the surface of the canvas, but Liquin is excellent for this purpose. Another alkyd medium, *Oleopasto,* has been developed specially for impasto work (see p. 27). It is designed to extend the paint and add body to it so that it can be applied in thick layers, with the brush or knife marks clearly visible.

BRUSHES AND KNIVES

Paint brushes for oil painting come in a wide range of shapes, sizes and materials. Good-quality brushes cost more, but are worth the initial outlay as they last longer and hold their shape better. For oils, unlike for watercolours, you need more than just one or two brushes, otherwise you will be forever cleaning them between applying one colour and the next. The ideal is to have one brush for each colour, but a selection of six should be enough to start off with.

The illustration shows the main shapes and types of brush:

Flats have long bristles with square ends. They hold a lot of paint and can be used flat, for broad areas, or on edge for fine lines.

Brights have shorter bristles than flats and produce strongly textured strokes. They are ideal for applying thick paint for impasto effects.

Rounds have long bristles, tapered at the ends. Like flats, they produce a wide variety of strokes, but they give a softer effect which is excellent for backgrounds, skies and portraits.

Filberts are fuller in shape than flats, with slightly rounded ends that make soft, tapered strokes.

Of the four types of brush, rounds and flats are the most useful to begin with. Brights and filberts can be added later, should you require them.

Each type of brush comes in a range of up to 12 sizes; so choose the size that best suits the style and scale of your paintings.

Hog's-hair bristles and sable hair are the traditional materials for oil-painting brushes; hog's hair is fairly stiff and holds the paint well, while sable gives a much smoother and less obvious brushstroke. Sables are very expensive indeed, but there are now several synthetic versions of the softer type of brush, and also mixtures of sable and synthetic. In the case of the soft brushes, you may need several or none at all, according to the way in which you work; some artists use nothing but soft nylon brushes and others nothing but hog's hair. The projects on pages 42 to 123 will give you an idea of the differing requirements of different styles.

Palette knives, made of flexible steel, are used for cleaning the palette and mixing paint, while painting knives are designed specifically for painting. The latter are unlikely to be needed by a beginner unless you have a particular desire to experiment with this kind of painting, but an ordinary straight-bladed palette knife should form part of your 'starter kit'.

PALETTES

Palettes come in a variety of shapes, sizes and materials, designed to suit your individual requirements. Thumbhole palettes are designed for easel painting. They have a thumbhole and indentation for the fingers, and the palette is supported on the forearm. Before buying a palette, try out different sizes and shapes to see which feels the most comfortable.

New wooden palettes should be treated by rubbing with linseed oil to prevent them absorbing the oil in the paint. You can even improvize your own palette, from any non-absorbent surface, making it any size and colour you like. An old white dinner plate might do, or a sheet of glass with white or neutral-coloured paper underneath it. Disposable palettes made of oil-proof paper are a boon for outdoor work, and remove the necessity for cleaning.

LEFT A selection of oil-painting brushes in both hog's hair and synthetic fibre. The four white (hog's-hair) brushes are the basic shapes: from left to right, flat, filbert, round and bright.

RIGHT A selection of palette and painting knives. Second from the left is the standard palette knife, which is designed mainly for cleaning the palette and mixing paint, but can also be used for applying paint to the support. The others are all specifically designed for painting. As with brushes, some experimentation is needed to find out which shape suits which individual; some artists never use painting knives at all.

PAINTBOXES

Theoretically, any old cardboard box will do to keep paints, brushes and media in, but if you are intending to carry paints around with you it is worth investing in a proper box with separate compartments for paints and brushes. Most of these are wooden, with a carrying handle, and are sold with their own palette which fits into the lid.

Alternatively you can improvize you own paintbox from a toolbox or fishing tackle box, which are less expensive and lighter to carry.

OIL PAINTING ACCESSORIES

Other essential items include dippers for your painting medium, which can be attached to the palette; jam jars or tin cans to hold white spirit for cleaning brushes; and of course a large supply of rags or kitchen paper (oil paint is very messy and needs to be cleaned up frequently).

Another useful painting aid is a mahl stick, which steadies your hand when you are painting small details or fine lines. The traditional mahl stick has a bamboo handle with a chamois cushion at one end. The stick is held across the canvas with the cushioned end resting lightly on a dry area of the painting, and you rest your painting arm on the stick to steady yourself as you paint. Mahl sticks are sold at artists' suppliers, but a piece of dowelling or garden cane with a bundle of rags tied to one end is quite adequate, and can be rested on the side of the canvas or board if the paint surface is wet. Page 65 shows a mahl stick being used.

For anyone who intends to do a lot of outdoor work, a pair of canvas separators is very useful. These are designed to keep two wet canvases apart without damaging the paint, and have a handle for carrying. It is necessary to have two canvases of the same size with you, even if you intend to use only one.

VARNISHES

Ideally, paintings should be varnished to protect them from dust and to restore the colours, which tend to become toned down as the paint dries. Many people associate varnish with that dark-brown, sticky look that was such a feature of Victorian paintings, but several clear synthetic varnishes are now available, both matt and gloss. Most varnishes, however, cannot be applied for at least six months, even a year if the paint is very thick, as it takes this long for it to dry out thoroughly. The exceptions are the temporary varnishes, such as retouching varnish, which can be applied when the paint is 'skin dry', that is, in about two weeks to a month. It can also be used to brush over an area that may have become dull and matt during the painting, as sometimes happens, and can be removed if necessary by rubbing gently with distilled turpentine.

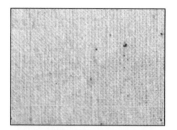

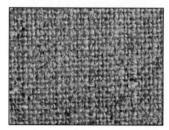

SUPPORTS

This is the term given to whatever surface is used to paint on, whether stretched canvas, hardboard or cardboard, paper – even a wall. The most commonly used support for oil painting is canvas, usually made of linen or cotton, and stretched to make it taut, but many other surfaces can be used, and each one has its own individual characteristics. Canvas provides a sympathetic surface and holds the paint well, while primed hardboard, favoured by some artists, is unyielding and holds the paint much less well, so that it tends to slip about. This can be an advantage for someone who paints with thinned – and thus quicker-drying – paint, and makes use of finely drawn detail, but is less suitable for thickly applied paint, as each successive layer will disturb the one below. You will certainly have to try several different supports before you can be sure which one suits you best, and even then you will probably find that different paintings call for different supports. The examples on pages 44 to 123 demonstrate the use of a great variety of types, and show how the artists have made use of particular surfaces to achieve the effects they wanted.

CANVAS

Canvases can be bought stretched and ready for use, but they are very expensive and it is much cheaper to stretch and prepare (prime) your own. Unprimed canvas can be bought by the metre in artists' suppliers, as can stretchers, which are sold in pairs so that any size can be made up. The illustration shows some different types of canvas, ranging from fine weave to very coarse. Generally, a coarse weave is suitable for broad, heavy brushwork, while a finely woven texture is best for finely detailed work. Linen canvas, which is undoubtedly the nicest surface to work on, is expensive and could be an unwise choice for a first attempt. Cotton canvas is much cheaper, and perfectly adequate. Cotton duck, in particular, stretches well because it has a tighter weave.

STRETCHING CANVAS

Stretching canvas is not at all difficult, and will save you money. To stretch a canvas you will need four wooden stretcher pieces – one for each side of the frame. In addition you will need 12-mm (½-in) carpet tacks to attach the canvas to the frame, a hammer and a pair of sharp scissors.

Assemble the stretchers, making sure that the assembled stretcher is square by measuring the diagonals – they should both be the same length. Then cut the canvas about 4 cm (1½ in) larger than the stretcher all round. Lay the stretcher frame on the canvas, then turn one edge of the canvas over the frame and tack or staple it in the centre of one side. Pull the opposite side of the canvas as firmly as possible and tack it at the centre of that side. Repeat this process on the other

ABOVE Stretchers can be bought in a wide variety of sizes. They are sold in pairs, which are then fitted together to form rectangles.

TOP Types of canvas. From left to right, top row: inexpensive cotton; good-quality cotton, which is similar to linen. MIDDLE ROW: hessian, very coarse and thus unsuitable for thinly applied paint or fine work, and linen. BOTTOM ROW: a different weave of linen and a ready-primed linen, suitable for most work and available from the larger artists' suppliers.

two sides, and continue tacking or stapling, working from the centre outwards, and placing the tacks about 2.5 cm (1 in) apart. Then fold in the corners and tack one over the other. Finally, tap in the wooden corner wedges (normally sold with the stretcher pieces) as far as necessary to tauten the canvas thoroughly. (These can be tapped in again later if the canvas loosens while you are working.)

An inexpensive method of stretching canvas is to stick it down on hardboard with glue size. This is rather a messy job, and does not provide such a pliable surface as stretched canvas, but it has one considerable advantage in that flat pieces of hardboard are much easier to store than canvases – an important consideration for anyone who has a space problem. There are two types of size, that sold in builders' merchants for preparing walls and so on, and animal-skin size, sold in most large artists' suppliers. The latter is the best choice, as it will probably be needed in any case for priming (see below), but it has slightly less sticking power than glue size. Cellulose and other adhesives should not be used as they could react with the oil paint. To prepare the size, which is sold in crystal form, first mix it with cold water in a proportion of about one of crystals to seven of water, and leave it for a short time until it has doubled in bulk. Heat it gently in an old saucepan or double-boiler (not one you will use for cooking) until all the crystals have melted thoroughly. Glue size can be allowed to boil, but animal-skin size should not, as this weakens it.

Cut the canvas to about 2.5 cm (1 in) larger all around than the hardboard, apply the hot size to the smooth side of the hardboard, lay the canvas on top and then go over it with a small, hard roller of the type sold for lino cuts to smooth out any creases. To fix the edges, simply turn them over the back of the hardboard and stick them down with more size. (This is the messiest part, as it must be done while the size is still warm and sticky.)

Any left-over size can be reheated and used again. This method is most suitable for the lighter types of canvas, as heavy linen will not stick thoroughly, and it can also be used for materials not actually sold for painting purposes, such as muslin or cotton lawn.

BOARDS AND PAPER

Hardboard is an inexpensive, strong yet lightweight support which you can buy from any timber yard or builders' suppliers. Either the smooth or the rough side can be used, the latter being suitable only for those who like to use their paint thick. Its disadvantage, which applies also to the canvas-covered hardboard described above, is that it warps, but if you are framing your work it can be straightened out at this stage by battening the back (sizing both sides of the board also helps to reduce warping). For a large painting, the hardboard can be battened first by either sticking or screwing two pieces of hardwood battening across the back. (If using screws, take care they do not come through to the front, as hardboard is quite thin.)

Prepared canvas boards can be bought from artists' suppliers in a variety of different surfaces, the more expensive ones being the best. The cheaper ones tend to have a rather coarse and greasy surface, but are probably adequate for a first attempt. Such boards are also prone to warping.

Paper and cardboard make perfectly satisfactory supports for oil painting as long as they are primed (see below). They are excellent for small, quick sketches, as the paper, being slightly absorbent, allows the paint to dry quite quickly. If using paper, buy a good-quality, heavy water-colour paper, as a thin paper will buckle when primed. Specially prepared paper, called oil sketching paper, can be bought, usually in pads. Some people get on well with this, but others find its surface greasy and unpleasant to work on, like that of the cheaper painting boards.

SIZING AND PRIMING

The conventional method of priming all supports is first to apply a coat of the animal-skin size described above, and when dry to apply a coat (or sometimes two) of oil-based primer. You can use ordinary household undercoat for this, but special oil primers are sold by artists' suppliers for the purpose, and are probably the wisest choice. However, oil primers do take a fairly long time to dry. An alternative is to use emulsion paint, which dries quickly, or the acrylic primer sold under the (incorrect) name of gesso, which is compatible with oil paint. Acrylic primer should always be applied direct to the canvas, without the preliminary coat of size, and two coats will usually be needed.

The purpose of sizing and priming is to provide a protective layer between the canvas and the oil paint. Some contemporary artists, among them the English artist Francis Bacon (b.1910), do paint on unprimed canvas in order to achieve special effects, but this should never be a general practice. The oil paint will eventually rot the canvas or other support, and the paint itself will dry out and flake off as all the oil will have been absorbed.

EASELS

An easel is a necessity. You may manage to produce one small painting by propping up your canvas on a table or shelf, but you will very soon find out how unsatisfactory this is. Without an easel you cannot adjust the height of your work – essential if you are doing a painting of a reasonable size, as you must be able to reach different areas of it easily and comfortably – and you cannot tilt the work, which you often need to do either to avoid light reflecting on its surface or to catch the best light for working.

There are several different types of easel on the market, from huge, sturdy studio easels to small sketching easels that are light and easily portable. Your choice will be dictated by the space in which you are working, whether you intend to work mostly indoors or outdoors, and by the size of your work and the type of painting you are doing. If you intend to work out of doors frequently you will need a sketching easel (though small sketches can be done by propping the canvas or board against the open lid of a paintbox). If, on the other hand, you know you are unlikely to paint anywhere but indoors, the heavier radial easel could be a good choice, but this cannot easily be dismantled and put away, so you might choose a portable easel for space reasons.

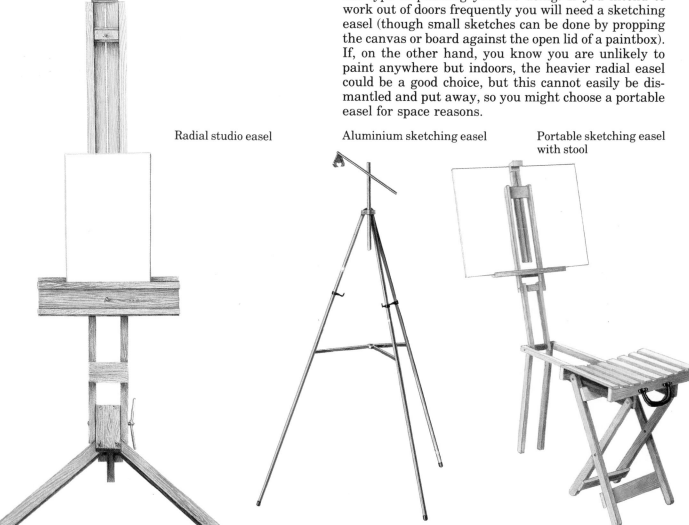

Radial studio easel

Aluminium sketching easel

Portable sketching easel with stool

There are three main types of sketching easel, the box easel, the wooden sketching easel and the aluminium sketching easel. The first type combines an easel and a paintbox, and can be folded up into a case for carrying. These were at one time very expensive, and the best ones still are, but cheaper versions are now appearing on the market, and for an outdoor painter they are a good choice, as everything can be carried in one piece of luggage.

Wooden sketching easels are inexpensive, but are not recommended, as the blocks which slide up and down in slots to enable you to adjust the height of the work tend to become warped, so that they either do not slide at all or are impossible to fix in position. There is nothing more infuriating than having to fight your easel, which often involves knocking it over, just when you want to work particularly fast because the light is changing.

The metal sketching easel, on the other hand, is excellent, and suffers from none of these disadvantages because metal cannot warp. It is easy to adjust, holds the work firmly, and has the additional advantage of being adjustable to a horizontal position for watercolours (you may find that you want to experiment with other media from time to time). It is also quite adequate for indoor work, providing you are not working on a vast scale, and can be tucked away unobtrusively in a corner when not in use.

The problem with all sketching easels except the heavier version of the box type is that because they are light, and thus easy to carry, they are also vulnerable to gusts of wind, the canvas or board acting as a most effective sail! Some artists manage to anchor their easel by pushing tent pegs into the ground and tying the easel legs to them, or by hanging a heavy stone from the centre of the easel.

THE WORKING SPACE

Few non-professional painters are fortunate enough to have access to a studio; nor indeed are all professional ones. Most people have to make do with a small, under-equipped room or just a corner of a room used by other people for other purposes. This can create problems, but these are surmountable with a little organization.

One problem is that oil paint is a messy medium and has an almost magical way of appearing on objects that seemed to be nowhere near it when you were painting. You get it on your hands without noticing, then you go and make a cup of coffee and it will be on the kettle, the mug, the spoon, and so on, ad infinitum. If you are working in a corner of a room, clean up as often as you can, including wiping your hands, never wander about with a loaded paintbrush, and cover the equipment table with plenty of newspaper.

A more serious problem is lighting. The best light for painting is, of course, daylight, but daylight is unpredictable and changes all the time, not only in variable weather conditions but also according to the time of day. If you have a north-facing window you are lucky, as north light (or south light if you live in the southern hemisphere) changes much less, but many rooms face east or west, in which case you will sometimes have the sun shining directly on to the work and reflecting off the paint surface, while at other times you will have almost no light at all.

Always try to position your easel so that the light source is behind you and coming over your left shoulder if you are right-handed.

Good light is vitally important: if you look in a good light at a painting done in a poor one you will see why. What were intended to be subtle gradations of colour and tone now appear as crude mixtures of bright colours and dingy ones, while what you thought of as nicely-blended, unobtrusive brushwork is actually quite clumsy and obvious.

One way of coping with this problem is to use artificial lighting which, while not as perfect as northerly daylight, is at least constant. The best lights for painting are the fluorescent 'daylight' ones, which can be bought either as ceiling lights or as lamps which can be fitted on to a shelf, table or windowsill. Look carefully at what is available before buying, as mistakes are expensive, and work out where the light source should be placed so that it does not reflect off the paint. One method is to fix a lamp over the window so that it boosts the available light, but a certain amount of trial and error may be involved before you arrive at a satisfactory solution.

Box easel

CHAPTER THREE

THE MECHANICS OF PAINTING

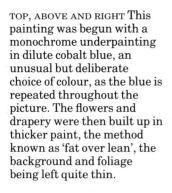

TOP, ABOVE AND RIGHT This painting was begun with a monochrome underpainting in dilute cobalt blue, an unusual but deliberate choice of colour, as the blue is repeated throughout the picture. The flowers and drapery were then built up in thicker paint, the method known as 'fat over lean', the background and foliage being left quite thin.

ALTHOUGH there are really no hard-and-fast rules in oil painting, it is helpful to have an idea of the various ways in which artists go about things so that you can experiment with different techniques, colour schemes and compositions as you evolve your own particular style. Rules are often useful in a negative way: once you know a rule you can break it for reasons of your own, or 'bend' it, as many artists have done with the rules of perspective. Constable and the French Impressionists broke the rules of their times, thus freeing painting from the very rigid set of procedures to which artists had previously been forced to adhere, but their knowledge of all the theories of painting was very thorough indeed.

GENERAL PAINTING TECHNIQUES

If you are painting a very simple subject, such as an empty landscape with a wide expanse of sky, there is often no need for an underdrawing or underpainting,

except perhaps a line or two to delineate the horizon. However, for a more complex subject such as a figure study, or perhaps a landscape including people or buildings, a preliminary drawing on the canvas is usually advisable. This enables you to work out the composition and the position of the main elements within it, and to plan the balance of dark colours and light ones. For a portrait or figure painting you will need to establish how you want to place the figure in relation to the background, and you will need to get the proportions of the figure right. If you start an ambitious painting with inadequate drawing you will be forever altering parts of it, which will not only spoil your enjoyment, but will also produce a laboured and overworked painting. Careful planning at the start enables you to be more spontaneous later.

Underdrawings can be done either in pencil or charcoal, the latter being preferable, as it is a broad medium, easier to use freely. To avoid loose charcoal mixing with the paint and muddying it, brush it down lightly with a rag before starting to paint – you will still retain the main lines of the drawing.

Underpainting – another form of drawing but done with a brush – can be made either in monochrome or an understated version of the finished colour scheme, in both cases using paint well thinned with turpentine. If you find a blank canvas somewhat intimidating, you will find that an underpainting overcomes the problem by providing a 'stepping-stone' from which you can build up the succeeding layers of colour with confidence.

A monochrome underpainting should concentrate on the main masses of light and shade, as in the example illustrated, and a coloured one should avoid bright and light colours, as you will want to build up to these as the painting progresses. Nowadays artists often use acrylic paint for underpainting, as this dries much faster than even thinned oil paint, enabling the next stage to proceed immediately.

A good general rule for oil painting – and a very old one – is to work 'fat over lean'. This simply means that in the initial stages the paint should be used fairly thin (diluted with turpentine only) becoming thicker and oilier as the painting progresses. Working in this way reduces the risk of the paint cracking as it dries out. If, however, 'lean' paint is brushed over a layer of 'fat' paint (containing a greater proportion of oil) what happens is that the lean layer dries first, and when the fat layer beneath it eventually starts to dry it contracts, causing the dry layer on top to crack.

Not all paintings, however, are done in stages in this way; many are completed at one sitting, with a minimum of drawing or underpainting or even none at all. This is known as *alla prima* painting, and is much used for landscape or quick portrait studies where the painter wants to record his impressions rapidly in a free and spontaneous manner. The paint is used thickly, with each colour laid down more or less as it will finally appear. When oil paints are used in this way, the colours blend into each other, particularly when one is laid on top of another. This is a feature of *alla prima* painting, known as working 'wet into wet', and was much exploited by the Impressionists, particularly Claude Monet (1840-1926) in his outdoor paintings. For anyone who has not used oils before, *alla prima* is a good way of starting, as it will give you an immediate 'feel' for the medium and force you to work fast without being over-conscious of each brushstroke.

SPECIAL PAINTING TECHNIQUES

As has been mentioned, there are many different ways of applying oil paint to create particular effects. Some of these are used almost unconsciously, when the painting seems to demand a particular approach, while others are the result of careful planning.

The method called *scumbling* comes into the first category and simply means applying semi-opaque

ABOVE This small painting was done by the *alla prima* method, with the paint used quite thickly and put down rapidly with little subsequent alteration.

The photograph (RIGHT) shows colours being blended into one another by working wet into wet. ABOVE a thin layer of transparent red paint is being laid over a dry layer of yellow. This is the technique called glazing, which gives an effect quite unlike that of one layer of thicker paint, as the colour below reflects back through the glaze, giving additional brilliance.

FAR LEFT The paint surface here is an important part of the painting, the broken patches and restless texture of the thickly applied colour enhancing the vividness of the subject. The paint was applied with a knife alone, and the detail, (LEFT), clearly shows how different is the effect from that of traditional brush painting.

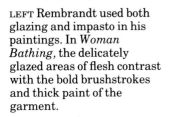

LEFT Rembrandt used both glazing and impasto in his paintings. In *Woman Bathing,* the delicately glazed areas of flesh contrast with the bold brushstrokes and thick paint of the garment.

RIGHT Here scumbling was used to suggest the texture of the chalk cliffs. The paint was scrubbed on with a brush over dry paint below, and in places was worked in with the fingers. The foreground was put on rather dry.

paint on top of another dry or semi-dry area of colour in an irregular way. Part of the layer below will show through, so that a 'broken' colour and texture is created. This can be very effective for particular parts of a painting, such as skies, rocks, tree trunks, fabric and so on. Anything can be used for putting on scumbled paint – stiff brushes, a rag or even the fingers – and the paint can be dragged, smudged or stippled.

Areas of irregular texture can be made by laying a flat area of colour in opaque paint and then 'blotting' it, when semi-dry, with non-absorbent paper such as pages from a glossy magazine. As you peel back the paper, it drags at the surface layer of paint and creates a stippled texture. This technique is called *frottage.*

A way of creating another kind of texture is *impasto,* in which the paint is laid on thickly, often with a palette knife. In the past, artists such as Rembrandt combined impasto with areas of delicate brushwork, pointing up the differences in texture between, for example, flesh and clothing. Today many artists use impasto as a technique on its own, building up heavy layers of paint to make a raised and densely-textured surface. Special painting mediums are available which

increase the bulk of the paint (see p. 15), and some artists even mix paint with sand for a rough, grainy surface.

Interesting effects can be achieved by drawing or scratching into a layer of wet oil paint to reveal another colour beneath or sometimes the white ground of the canvas, as in the example illustrated. The implement used can be anything pointed, such as the end of the brush handle or a knitting needle. This method is called *sgraffito.*

A technique that comes into the deliberate planning category is *glazing,* in which thin, transparent paint is laid over an area of already dry paint. Layers of glazes can be built up one over the other to create effects akin to the deep glow of wood that has been lovingly polished – but glazing is not a quick method as each layer must dry before the next is applied. Many of the rich, glowing colours used by artists of the past, such as Titian, were produced by laying thin glazes of brilliant colour over an underpainting, and the luminous quality of the landscapes painted by J. W. M. Turner (1775–1851) are the result of layers of glazing over thick, pale impastos.

ABOVE The artist scratches through the paint with a palette knife to reveal the white surface of the canvas. Where there are several layers in a painting, the technique can also be used to reveal one or more of the colours below.

LEFT The still life was given sparkle as well as additional definition by the use of the sgraffito technique.

These thumbnail sketches, of female figures in various poses against different backgrounds, illustrate the way in which some artists try out possible compositions for paintings. Such drawings, which can be done quite quickly and need be little more than scribbles, are an excellent means of working out the arrangement of the main shapes and the balance of lights and darks.

COMPOSING A PICTURE

The word 'composition' has a slightly alarming ring to it – it sounds as though it might be an intellectual exercise quite beyond the capabilities of the ordinary person. This really is not so: composing a painting is mainly a question of selecting, arranging and re-arranging, just as you might do when deciding on the decor for a room or when taking a photograph. A large, complex painting with numerous people and objects in it does, of course, need some thought; otherwise there may be too much activity in one part of the picture and not enough in another. But even here, it is less a matter of following a prescribed set of rules than of working out the balance of the various shapes, as in the case of planning a room – no one would put all the furniture crowded together on one side and leave the rest empty.

A 'good composition' is one in which there is no jarring note, the colours and shapes are well-balanced, and the picture as a whole seems to sit easily within its frame or outer borders. Even a simple head-and-shoulders portrait is composed, and a vital part of composition is selection – what you put in and what you leave out. In the case of a portrait you will need to establish whether the person should be seated, and if so on what, whether you want to include the chair, whether you want the hands to form part of the composition, and whether you want to use something in the background, for example part of a window frame, to balance the figure.

If you are painting a landscape you may think composition is not involved, that you are just painting what you see, but you will have chosen a particular view, just as you would when taking a photograph, and in choosing it you will have gone at least some way towards composing it. You may then find that you want to exaggerate or re-arrange some feature in the foreground, such as a rock or a tree, to provide extra interest, or alter the bend of a path to lead the eye into the picture.

There are some basic errors which should be avoided if possible. In general it is not a good idea to divide a landscape horizontally into two equal halves – the land and the sky – as the result will usually be monotonous. A line, such as a path or fence, should not lead directly out of the picture unless balanced by another line which leads the eye back into it. A still-life or portrait should not be divided in half vertically, while a flower painting is unlikely to be pleasing to the eye if the flower arrangement is placed too far down in the picture area, too far to one side, or very small in the middle, with a large expanse of featureless background.

In the case of interiors, portraits, still-lifes and flowers, backgrounds can be used as a device to balance the main elements of the composition. Use part of a piece of furniture behind a seated figure, for example, or a subtly patterned wallpaper which echoes or contrasts with the main shapes and colours in the figure. In landscape painting the sky is a vital part of the composition, and should always be given as much care and thought as the rest of the painting.

Even if you are working quickly, it is often helpful to make some drawings, known as *thumbnail sketches* (though they need not be small) before you start on the painting. These may consist of just a few roughly-drawn lines to establish how the main shapes can be placed, or they may help you to work out the tonal pattern of the composition.

A viewing frame is equally useful, particularly for landscapes painted on the spot. When faced with a large expanse of land and sky the problem is always how much of it to paint, where to start and finish, and how much of what you see will actually fit on the canvas. Anyone who takes photographs will be familiar with this problem: you raise your camera at a splendid view only to find that the small section of it you can see through the viewfinder is quite dull and featureless. A viewing frame is simply a rectangular aperture cut in a piece of card – a good size is about 11.5 × 15.25 cm (4½ × 6 in) – which you hold up in front of you to frame and isolate the subject. Once you have chosen the particular area of landscape that interests you, you can then decide how you want to

ABOVE The natural inclination when painting subjects like trees is to try and get everything in, but in this painting the artist has allowed the foreground trees to 'bust' out of the frame, giving a stronger and more exciting effect.

treat it and how much re-arranging is needed to make an interesting composition.

A useful aid for indoor work is a polaroid camera; several photographs of the subject taken from different angles and with different backgrounds will give you an idea of how you can best approach the painting, and they will also help you to work out the balance of colours and tones.

COLOUR AND LIGHT

Colour can be a very complex subject indeed – whole books have been written on colour theory. Such theory is beyond the scope of this book, and in any case would be more likely to be a hindrance than a help to an inexperienced painter, but there are some basic guidelines which will help you to make a picture work, and there are also some terms which you will need to understand.

Colour has two main qualities, tone and intensity, the first being the darkness or lightness of a particular colour and the second being its brightness. If you take a black-and-white photograph of a landscape composed entirely of greens, you will see that some appear darker than others – proving that a single colour can have dark tones and light tones. In the same landscape, some of the greens will be brighter and more vibrant than others – in other words, more intense.

Colours which are opposite one another on the colour wheel, such as red and green, yellow and violet,

RIGHT In this painting the contrast between the dark and light tree trunks has been emphasised by the use of very thin paint. The solid foliage of the evergreens draws attention to the slenderness of the foreground trunks and provides a counterpoint.

are called *complementary colours*. These can be used in a deliberate way to balance and 'spark off' one another; for example, a small area of bright red in a landscape could be used to enhance and intensify a large expanse of green. The Op painters of the 1960s used complementary colours in a highly intellectual way: by juxtaposing complementaries of the same hue and tone they created restless, 'jumping' effects.

Colours are basically either 'warm' or 'cool', and the warm ones will tend to 'advance', or push themselves to the front of a painting, while the cool ones will recede. In general, the warm colours are the reds, yellows, bright yellow-greens and oranges, while cool ones are the blues and colours with blue in them, such as blue-green. Some blues, however, are warmer than others, and some reds are cooler than others. You can see this by placing ultramarine or cerulean blue (both quite warm) next to Prussian or Antwerp blue (both cool), and alizarin crimson (cool) next to cadmium red (warm).

You can make use of the 'advancing' and 'retreating' qualities of warm and cool colours in modelling forms and in creating a sense of space and depth. In portrait painting, for example, use warm colours for the prominent areas such as the nose, chin and cheekbones, and cool colours for receding or shadowed areas such as underneath the chin. In landscapes, use warm colours in the foreground and cool, bluish tones in the background to emphasize the feeling of receding space (see below).

There is no colour without light, and the direction, quality and intensity of light constantly changes and modifies colours. This fact became almost an obsession with the Impressionist painter Claude Monet; he painted many studies of the same subject – a group of haystacks – at different times of the day in order to understand and analyze these changes. You can see the effects very easily for yourself if you look at any scene – the view from a window or a corner of the garden – first on a cloudy morning and then in low evening sunlight. In the evening everything will suddenly become golden and a brick wall which might have appeared a drab brown in the morning may now be a bright hue of orange or pink.

Light is vital to a painting, whether a landscape or a still-life or portrait study, and the way it falls defines the shape of objects and determines their colour. Both photographers and painters of landscape know that the high midday sun is their enemy, as it creates dense patches of shadow and drains the landscape of colour and definition. A portrait or still-life can also look flat, dead and colourless if lit directly from above, while a side light can suddenly bring it to life, creating exciting shadow areas of purple or green and vivid, sparkling highlights.

AERIAL PERSPECTIVE

This is a way of using colour and tone to give a sense of space in a painting, and to indicate recession. It is

particularly important in landscape painting. If you look at an expanse of landscape, such as one with fields and trees in the foreground and distant hills or mountains beyond, you will see that the colours become paler and cooler in the distance, with details barely visible. The objects in the foreground will be brighter and have much clearer areas of contrast, or tonal differences, which will become smaller in the middle distance and may disappear altogether in the far distance, so that the hills or mountains appear as pure areas of pale blue. It takes some experience to use aerial perspective successfully; if you accidentally mix a rather warm blue on your palette and try to use it for the distant hills you will find that they seem almost to jump forward to the front of the picture. The same applies if you combine a pale colour with a much darker one; there will then be a greater tonal difference than is actually present and the background will begin to vie with the foreground.

Aerial perspective can, of course, be either exploited or ignored. Sometimes, for instance, you might be more interested in creating a flat pattern or you might want simply to use areas of vivid colour.

LINEAR PERSPECTIVE

This, like colour theory, can be a very complex subject, almost a science. During the Renaissance, when the laws of perspective were first being formulated in a systematic way, artists vied with one another to produce more and more elaborate perspective drawings; for example Paolo Uccello (*c*.1396-1475) made a study of a chalice broken down into a series of separate receding surfaces which is quite breathtaking in its intricacy. However, unless your particular interest is architecture – you might perhaps want to make a series of detailed studies of the interiors of churches, for instance – it is most unlikely that you will need to understand more than the most basic rules, which are helpful when faced with the problem of how to make buildings look solid or how to indicate that they are being viewed from above.

Theoretically, you can make perspective work by just drawing what you see, and some art teachers believe that such rules should not be learnt, at any rate by beginners, as they have a stultifying effect. This is certainly true to some extent; too much careful pondering over the precise angle of parallel lines can

BELOW A scene such as this relies on some understanding of the laws of perspective or the effect of the high-perched buildings would be lost. When sketching out of doors, it is often helpful to mark in a horizon line so that the angles can be related to it; the eye alone cannot always judge such angles truthfully.

RIGHT One-, two- and three-point perspective. In the first, only two planes can be seen, and thus the parallel lines have the same vanishing point. When three planes are visible, two separate vanishing points are needed, and if the same cube is seen from above or below the horizon the sides will also converge at a third vanishing point.

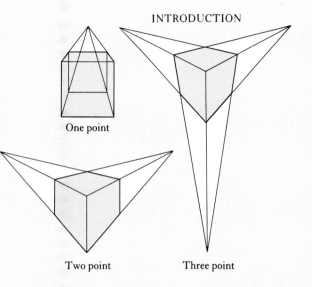

INTRODUCTION

One point

Two point

Three point

horizon line

turn a painting which could have been fresh and immediate into one which is correct but dull. However, few amateur artists possess the enviable gift of being able to turn direct observation into drawing or painting with any degree of ease, and a knowledge of the basic rules can have a liberating effect rather than the reverse, as long as you don't allow yourself to become too bound up in them.

The primary rule, which many people learn at school, is that all receding parallel lines meet at a vanishing point, which is on the horizon. It is easy enough to learn such rules, but far less easy to apply them. A single building has several different planes, or sets of parallel lines, and a group of buildings, such as a farmhouse with barns and outhouses, has even more, as the buildings are often set at random angles to one another. Where, you may ask yourself, is this horizon at which they will all meet, and how is it determined? This is dependent on your chosen viewpoint. If you are high up, on a cliff or hilltop, the horizon will be level with you, so that you have very little sky and a large expanse of land or sea. You will be looking down at the group of buildings, and the

parallel lines receding from you will slope up to the horizon. If you are at a low angle, perhaps sitting on the ground, the horizon, still at eye-level, will also be low, giving a large expanse of sky. The buildings will be above the horizon and the receding parallels will slope down to it.

In the case of parallels running directly away from you, the vanishing point would be within the picture area, but for different planes at angles to them it will be a hypothetical one which can be some way outside the picture area to the right or left. If you are painting out of doors, the viewing frame previously mentioned is helpful in establishing where the various lines are leading to, or a small pocket ruler can be held up in front of your eye and lined up with a rooftop.

Of course, many artists choose either to ignore or to exaggerate the rules of perspective so as to create their own personal effects. For example, an artist who is more interested in the patterns suggested by a particular scene might paint the buildings quite flat, with no perspective at all, as a child would, while another might choose to 'see' a subject from above, with the horizon so high that there is no sky area at all.

CHAPTER FOUR
STARTING
TO
PAINT

IF you have never painted at all, or if you have not used a particular medium before, the idea of making a start can be quite daunting. If you are intending to go to a painting class, it is less alarming, as you will be painting what is put in front of you to paint, and a teacher will be on hand to advise, but if you are working at home there will be a great many decisions to make. For instance, what will you paint, what size will you work, and how will you actually begin? This chapter provides some suggestions and guidelines to help build up your confidence and so increase your enjoyment of painting.

CHOOSING A SUBJECT

Many people seem to feel that, just as there are 'proper' ways of going about a painting, there are also 'proper' subjects. This is quite untrue; as we have seen, there is no way of applying oil paint that is more correct than another, nor is there any one subject that makes a better painting than another. Nudes, still-lifes, flowers and landscapes are all types of painting hallowed by long tradition, but many artists have made fine paintings of just the corner of a room, a wall with a few flowers against it or a single tree. Vincent van Gogh made deeply moving and expressive still-lifes from such subjects as a pair of peasant's boots or a pile of books on a table.

Still-life did not exist as a painting subject until the Dutch artists of the 17th century 'invented' it. Nor was landscape, except as a background to a figure or group of figures, acceptable until the late 18th and early 19th centuries. In the past, the subject of a painting was largely dictated by the demands of patrons, but we have no such restrictions.

It should be said, however, that some subjects are more difficult than others, and it can be discouraging to find you have set yourself a task which your experience is not equal to. Portraits, for example, are particularly difficult. You have to cope with so many problems: how to render the colour of flesh, the texture of hair and clothing, the way the light falls on the planes of the face and, finally, how to 'get a likeness'. If your interests do lie in this direction, you could start with a self-portrait, as in this way you will have total control over your 'sitter' and can work at your own speed without feeling rushed and flustered. You will know your own face well already.

Still-lifes, flowers and landscapes all provide good starting points, depending on your particular interests. Subjects for still-lifes can be found in most people's homes or the nearest vegetable or flower shop, and you can choose your own arrangement, light it in any way you want and take your time over it. In the case of landscape, if the weather is not suitable for outdoor painting, or if you feel shy about it, you could start by working from a photograph (but beware of trying to 'copy' it in exact detail) or you could paint the view from a window.

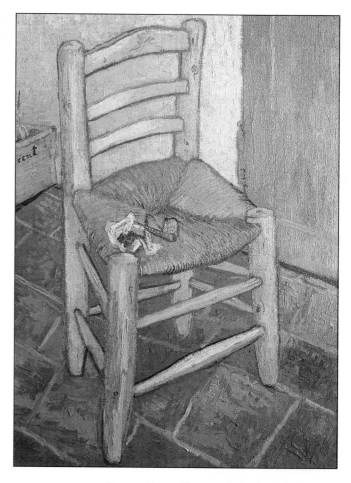

ABOVE AND RIGHT Domestic interiors have been a favourite subject with artists since the Dutch 17th-century masters. These two paintings, Van Gogh's Yellow Chair and Gwen John's A Corner of the Artist's Room in Paris, although totally different in their treatment and handling of colour and paint, both give a strong feeling of serenity, just as the Dutch paintings did.

Lighting plays a vital part in the arrangement of a still life, flower painting or portrait, and a subject can change quite dramatically according to the way it is lit. Back lighting (TOP LEFT) can be very effective for flowers, as the light will shine through the petals in places, giving a brilliant sparkle, with the front foliage and vase appearing very dark. Front lighting (ABOVE LEFT) tends to make any subject seem flat and dull, while side or diagonal lighting (TOP AND ABOVE RIGHT) will define the forms more clearly.

CHOOSING A SHAPE AND SIZE

This may seem trivial, but in fact both shape and size have an important part to play in the composition and treatment of a painting. A panoramic landscape, for instance, may suggest a wide horizontal shape which will enable you to show the broad sweep of the land as well as giving a sense of peace and tranquility. A single tree might call for a narrow vertical painting, while a still-life with a lot of objects in it could suggest a rather square one.

Size is a very personal matter: some artists work on vast canvases too big to fit in most living-rooms, while others produce tiny, detailed work on supports no larger than the average photograph. If you are working at home you are unlikely to want to work on a very large scale, and it is not usually a good idea to start very small. A good starting size is about 51 × 40.6 cm (20 × 16 in), a standard one in which you can buy both boards and canvases.

Painting is rather like handwriting – people with large writing feel constricted if for any reason they are forced to write small, and if your 'natural size' for painting is much larger than the support you have chosen you will soon find out, as your painting will seem to spread of its own volition beyond the edges. Until you have established a size which suits you, it is wise to use an inexpensive support, such as a piece of primed paper or cardboard, oil sketching paper or 'canvas board'. Hardboard is not recommended for early attempts as it has a slippery surface which can give a messy and unmanageable paint surface.

AVOIDING DISCOURAGEMENT

If your painting goes wrong at an early stage you are bound to feel depressed and discouraged. Various suggestions are given here which will help you to avoid or overcome the more common problems.

TINTING THE GROUND

Starting to paint on a glaring expanse of white canvas can be quite daunting, but even more important is the fact that a white surface is also 'dishonest', as it prevents you from judging the tones and colours correctly. There is very little pure white in nature, as white, like any other colour, is always modified by the light or shadow falling on it. Also, no colour exists in a particular way except in relation to the colours surrounding it. Thus, if you start a flower painting by putting down a bold brushstroke of pure cadmium red on a white canvas it will almost certainly be wrong, as the red you are seeing is actually given its quality by its relationship to the background, which may be neutral or even dark.

A method often used by artists is to tint the canvas in a neutral colour, usually a warm brown or grey, before starting the painting. This can be done either by mixing pigment in with the primer or by putting a wash of oil paint, such as raw umber, heavily diluted

ABOVE Although still-life and flower arrangements need not be elaborate, some thought is needed in the initial setting up if the foreground and background are not to become dull and featureless. Thumbnail sketches and polaroid photographs are useful aids in setting up an arrangement.

ABOVE The subject of this simple still-life was the artist's collection of assorted bottles, with the fruit used as a balance to the colours and texture of the glass. The lighting was entirely natural, simply the side-light coming in through a window, but the objects were set up with care so that the shadows fell pleasingly.

ABOVE These drawings show the different elements of a still-life arranged in a variety of ways. A symmetrical arrangement (LEFT) tends to be monotonous, but the arrangement, with the flat plane of the table angled away from the eye and a more varied grouping of the fruit (CENTRE), has considerably more visual interest. The drawing of the flower and fruit with draperies (RIGHT) provides more linear contrast and a busier background.

with turpentine, over the white ground. Acrylic paint can also be used for this since it dries much faster than oil paint, and you could buy a single tube just for this purpose. But remember that acrylic paint should not be used over an oil ground; oil can be used over acrylic, but acrylic cannot be used over oil.

PREPARATION

Always start with an adequate drawing or underpainting (see p. 24) in order to place the main design elements in the way you want them. Even a simple subject such as bowl of fruit can go very wrong if you fail to judge correctly the size of the fruit in relation to the bowl, or the bowl in relation to the table it is standing on. You may be impatient to start on the real business – the laying on of paint – but it does pay to take your time at this stage, for it will avoid a lot of frustration later.

KEEPING THE PICTURE MOVING

Try to avoid working in detail on one part of the painting at the expense of others. This approach can lead to a disjointed-looking painting, since you are more likely to tire of it half-way through. Generally, it is better to work on all parts of the canvas at once, so that you have a better idea of how one part relates to another in colour, tone and texture.

Some artists, such as the English painter Stanley Spencer (1891-1959), successfully reversed this process by starting with a careful and detailed pencil drawing and then painting area by area. There is theoretically nothing wrong with working in this way, but an inexperienced painter is unlikely to have the very clear vision of the finished painting which is required for such an approach.

In general, it is easiest to build up oil paint light over dark, as white is the most opaque colour; so keep to dark and middle tones in the early stages, working up gradually to the light and bright tones and colours. Always try to see the background as part of the painting, not just as an unimportant area; even a plain white wall has colours in it, and a totally flat background can be used as a shape, to form part of the composition. Avoid getting bogged down in detail too early; fine lines, such as the stems of flowers or small facial details in a portrait, are best left until last.

PROBLEM-SOLVING

Even paintings by professionals go wrong, but the beauty of oil paint is that they can so easily be altered. If you suddenly notice that your drawing is incorrect and that you have quite misunderstood a shape or colour, the best course is not to try to overpaint, but to scrape off the area with a palette knife and then repaint it. You may even decide to scrape down the whole painting and start more or less from scratch – this is often more satisfactory than trying to alter each individual area only to find that something is still not right. If you find that the surface of the painting has

Different artists have different methods of making sketches, according to their individual style and what particular aspect of a scene they want to note and remember. Some do detailed drawings in pen and ink or pen and wash, some make rough pencil sketches with colour notes, while others use oil paint, which is an excellent sketching medium because it can be applied so quickly.

become so overloaded with paint that you are just churning it up by continuing to add layers, there is a useful method, invented by a painting teacher called Henry Tonks and named *tonking* after him. This is done by laying a sheet of absorbent paper, such as newspaper, over the painting, rubbing it gently and removing it; this takes off the top layer of paint, and leaves you with something similar to a coloured under-painting.

USING REFERENCE MATERIAL

Painting is about looking at things – a good painter is constantly assessing objects and scenes with a view to translating them into paintings. This kind of analytical vision is largely a matter of habit and training – the more interested in painting you are the closer you will look and the more you will see – but few people have perfect visual memories, and for this reason artists often make visual references to use later on. Normally these take the form of sketches, and art students are always urged to carry sketchbooks at all times. Even a small, rough pencil sketch, sometimes with notes made about the quality of the light and the colours in the scene, can be turned into a complete landscape painting, or sometimes several sketches are made for different parts of a planned painting. For instance, a view of boats in a harbour might call for a rough overall sketch and some additional, more detailed drawings of individual boats.

It is certainly a good idea to carry a sketchbook – it is good practice if nothing else – but it takes some degree of skill to produce drawings which are good enough to provide all the information you may need and it takes experience to know what it is you actually want to make such 'notes' about. Photographs are now much used for this purpose, either as alternatives to sketches or as additions to them, and some artists even use picture postcards, either to suggest a theme for a painting or to remind them of some forgotten detail. One advantage of photographs is that they can record fleeting impressions, such as the sparkle of light on water, or a dramatic purple-grey sky just before a storm. They are also very useful for portrait painting, since few people are able to stay in one position long enough for a complete painting to be done.

However, photographs should be used with caution, and treated as aids to painting rather than models to copy. Straight copies of photographs, either of landscapes or people, can look very dull and dead, missing either the sparkle of the original scene or the character of the person. If you are using photographs for landscape painting, try to use several rather than just one, combining elements from each. Make a rough sketch from them and work from this rather than direct from the photographs. For portraits, they are generally used as a back-up, with the initial stages of the painting being done from life. The photographs can then be used for details, such as hands and clothing, with perhaps another live sitting for the final stage.

CHAPTER FIVE

OUTDOOR

SUBJECTS

ALL the paintings on the following pages, although very different from one another, fall into the broad category of landscape, a term which can really be used to describe any subject that is located outside the walls of the studio or home, even if it is a painting of a building or a single tree. Outdoor subjects such as these need not actually be painted out of doors – indeed many fine landscapes are painted in a studio – but at some stage in the inspiration and evolution of a good landscape, close observation of the outdoor world is vital. Outdoor subjects thus present challenges and problems very different from those of still-lifes or portraits: the painter of landscapes cannot arrange the subject and lighting as he chooses; he can only decide on a scene and then select what he wants to show and what he will leave out. One painter, for instance, may be particularly interested in the way the light falls on a particular scene, or in the ever-changing shapes and colours of the clouds, while another will ignore these aspects in favour of shapes or flat patterns.

A FARMHOUSE IN DERBYSHIRE

THIS painting was done from one of several sketches made on the spot. As you can see, the sketch is quite a rough one, but it provides all the necessary information as the subject is fairly simple and has been treated broadly, with little detail. When doing sketches specifically for paintings, rather than just sketching for its own sake, it is necessary to have some idea of how the finished painting will look, or you may find you have not made the 'notes' you will need. For example, if the artist had intended to treat the buildings in a much more precise and detailed way he probably would have needed to make more sketches of particular aspects of the building.

The composition has been somewhat altered in the painting, to make the path more central, and the gatepost has been exaggerated to create a sense of space between it and the farmhouse. The composition is simple and effective, with the curves of the lane and fence leading the eye in to the buildings, which are the focal point of the picture. This compositional device of a curve leading in to a central point is much used by landscape painters. The horizon is quite high, with the sky broken up into a rough triangle by the lines of the trees descending on each side of the building, and the sky itself echoes the line of trees on the right.

The painting was done very quickly, almost as it might have been if done on the spot, and the hardboard used as the support was first tinted with thinned acrylic paint in a shade of yellow ochre. This coloured ground has been allowed to show through in places in the finished painting, giving it a warm glow. This could not have been done on a white ground, as patches of white showing would be distracting and would throw all the colours off balance. Yellow ochre was chosen in this case because the painting was planned in shades of yellow and warm green, but for a different subject, a cool seascape, for example, a blue or grey ground might be used.

A charcoal underdrawing was done first to establish the main lines of the composition, after which thinned paint was used to block in the main areas. The paint became thicker as the painting progressed, with each area being worked on at the same time, so that the picture quickly began to emerge as a whole rather than as a series of bits – sky, foreground, middle distance and so on. When painting the buildings, the artist applied paint that was only roughly mixed on the palette, so that each brushstroke actually contained several colours. (Buildings can look flat and unreal if painted in too regular a way.) In the case of the trees, wet paint was applied on top of another still-wet layer (known as 'wet into wet'), thus modifying the colours and giving an impression of leafy texture. Quite a limited palette was used: three greens, three yellow-browns and one blue, plus black and white. Some artists disapprove of black and do not use it at all, but it is useful in landscape painting as it can be mixed with yellow to produce particularly rich greens.

1

2

TOP **1** A rough underdrawing was done with charcoal to establish the main lines. Pencil could have been used instead, or similar lines drawn with a brush and diluted paint, but pencil tends to mix with and muddy the paint, while a brush drawing takes a while to dry sufficiently to enable the first layer of paint to be put on. Charcoal can either be sprayed with fixative before the paint is applied or 'knocked back' by gently flicking with a rag to remove the surplus.

BELOW OPPOSITE **2** AND RIGHT **3** The main areas of colour were quickly blocked in with thinned paint and a medium-sized flat brush. This shape of brush should not be used for scrubbing on paint – a round one is best for this – but for more sweeping strokes.

BELOW **4** The picture began to emerge as a whole entity, as paint was applied loosely all over the surface at the same time. The colours used became slightly modified and defined as the painting progressed, but the basic balance of lights and darks was established at this stage.

3

4

5

ABOVE **5** AND RIGHT **6** The
paint was used more thickly
as the painting progressed,
the steps at the side of the
house being put in last with
thick paint and a small
brush. Details such as this,
and the fence and gatepost,
were left until the final
stages, and add a crisp
definition to the painting.
Note how the yellow ground
has been allowed to show
through the loosely applied
paint behind the house,
echoing the golden colour of
the path and giving a unity
to the whole picture.

6

MATERIALS USED

- Support: hard-
  board 60.7 × 91.4
  cm (24 × 36 in)
  primed with
  acrylic primer and
  tinted with acrylic
  yellow ochre
- Brushes: flats and
  brights, numbers
  5, 7 and 10
- Colours: ivory
  black, titanium
  white, permanent
  green, sap green,
  chrome green,
  yellow ochre, raw
  sienna, burnt
  sienna and
  ultramarine

THE HEADLAND

THIS painting shows oil paint being used in a way more often associated with watercolour – in very thin washes. The paint was diluted so much that it was virtually transparent, and each wash was allowed to dry before the next was applied. Since oil paint mixed with a medium such as linseed oil can take a very long time to dry, turpentine was used in combination with the fast-drying alkyd medium, Liquin, which binds the pigment as well as thinning it; if turpentine had been used alone the paint would simply have dribbled down the surface.

If you look at the photograph of the scene you may see why the painter has chosen to work in this way; it is an extremely linear and angular subject, with the group of trees starkly defined against the sky and the very distinct lines of the cliffs converging at the bottom. Using paint thickly, in a more conventional manner, would have given an effect much softer than the one created in this picture.

Using oil paint in this way requires a rather deliberate approach – again much more like a watercolour technique – and the painting was begun with a very careful drawing in pencil. The colour scheme is deliberately sombre, with only six colours being used in all, but although the palette is so limited the colours are neither dull nor muddy, with the blue of the sea appearing quite bright in the context of the surrounding greys and greens. The sky, which the photograph shows as containing two distinct areas of tone, has been painted almost, but not quite, as a flat area, thus allowing the eye to concentrate on what is really important – the cliff itself. Painting the clouds as they actually appeared would have detracted from the effect rather than enhancing it. This kind of selection and rejection of elements is an important part of landscape painting.

The support chosen for the painting was a tall, narrow one, which suits the vertical emphasis of the subject. The surface of the canvas board shows through in places, and additional texture has been introduced by drawing with a pencil on top of the paint to define the lines of the cliffs, by scratching into the paint with a scalpel and by spattering thinned paint on to the board to suggest the appearance of the shingle beach.

1

ABOVE **1** A detailed and precise underdrawing was made with a sharp 3B pencil, after which the first diluted wash of olive green paint was carefully laid down on the area at the top of the cliff.

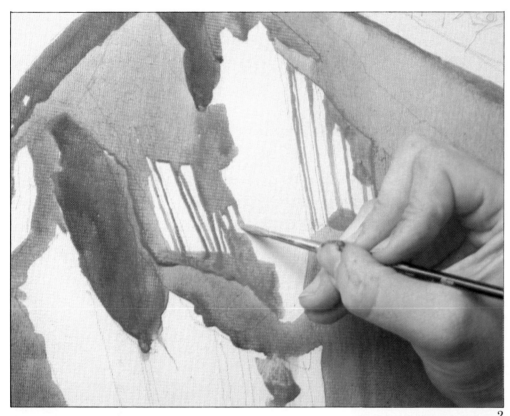

LEFT **2** More thinned paint was applied with a fine, soft brush, with areas of white being left uncovered. The lines were painted very carefully as this technique does not allow changes to be made. The pencil lines of the original drawing show through the thin paint, but this is not a disadvantage as in this case it adds to the effect.

BELOW RIGHT **4** The same pencil used for the original drawing was now used to draw into the paint to create the effect of the rocky fissures in the cliff face. As the paint is so thin the pencil lines are quite distinct; pencil marks in thicker paint would create indentations similar to those made by scratching with a knife.

2

4

LEFT **3** The trees and the wall below them were painted almost as flat areas with a fine sable brush. The painter could safely rest his hand on the painting while doing this detailed work as the paint in that area was already dry.

3

5

6

7

MATERIALS USED

- Support: fine-grained, ready-primed canvas board 76.2 × 50.8 cm (30 × 20 in)
- Brushes: number 6 sable and a number 6 soft synthetic as well as two flat bristle brushes, numbers 4 and 7
- Colours: titanium white, ivory black, cobalt blue, Payne's grey and yellow ochre, thinned with turpentine and Liquin

8

9

TOP LEFT **5** The support has now been fully covered, but areas of white have been left unpainted, to be treated in a different way in the final stages. The edges which separate each area of colour from the next are sharp and clearly defined at this stage; no blending has yet been done.

The detail (TOP RIGHT **6**) shows wet paint being applied to the dark area below the cliff. A crumpled tissue was used to create texture.

CENTRE RIGHT **7** To suggest the shingled beach, diluted paint was spattered on to the support with a stiff brush.

ABOVE LEFT **8** A scalpel was used to scratch into the paint, allowing fine lines of white to show through, a technique known as *sgraffito*.

ABOVE **9** This detail shows thicker paint in a mixture of white and Payne's grey being used for highlights. The paint was then blended with the finger.

IN THE GARDEN

THIS painting of a corner of a town garden, while falling within the general category of landscape, is actually more of an 'outdoor still-life', and it illustrates very well the statement made earlier that subjects for paintings can be found virtually anywhere. If you put two or three people into the same garden and told them to do a painting of some aspect of it, they would probably all choose quite different ones, depending on their particular interest and way of looking at things. This particular artist chose a subject which was literally under his feet, because he was attracted to the colours and patterns of the flagstones, the lines of the pot and stakes, and the texture of the foliage.

The painting was done out of doors in circumstances of some difficulty – the weather, and therefore the light, was changeable – and the painting had to be completed under an umbrella. A comparison of the finished painting with the photograph shows two things: firstly how the camera flattens out both colour and perspective, and secondly how various selections, rejections and adjustments have been made by the artist in order to make a satisfying composition. The foliage in the background, for instance, has been reduced to a few telling brushstrokes (if treated in more detail they could have detracted from the foreground); the colours of the flagstones have been altered and lightened to allow the foreground foliage to stand out, and the line of the stake has been altered so that it neither cuts the pot in half nor conflicts with the lines of the flagstones.

The painting had to be done quickly as the weather was so unpredictable, and the composition was established rapidly by blocking in the main areas in thinned paint. This degree of certainty about the way a finished painting should look is largely the result of years of observation and practice, but even professional artists sometimes change their minds, and as the painting progressed it became necessary to make some alterations. In the first detail you can see that the line of the stake ran exactly parallel to the line of the flagstone on the right, and led the eye of the viewer out of the picture, which should always be avoided. Thus the artist decided to change it, bringing the stake further over. Once this alteration was done, the paint was built up more thickly over the original thinned colour – in one place it was even smudged on with the fingers – and the paint surface in the finished picture is richly textured, particularly in the foreground area, where the brushstrokes have been used in a directional way to suggest individual leaves.

Paint surface is extremely important and plays a more vital part than many people realize in the finished effect of a painting; however well-chosen the colours and however good the drawing and composition may be, an unpleasant, slimy or churned-up paint surface will detract from the picture and may even make it impossible to see its virtues.

1

ABOVE **1** No drawing was done on the support as time was so limited, and the main areas were blocked in quickly with diluted paint. It became obvious very soon that the line of the stake would have to be changed, and this was done with masking tape, a useful addition to the painter's tools. Two parallel lines of tape were laid down to define the new line, and colour was applied rapidly right over it. The tape was then removed, leaving a clear, well-defined line.

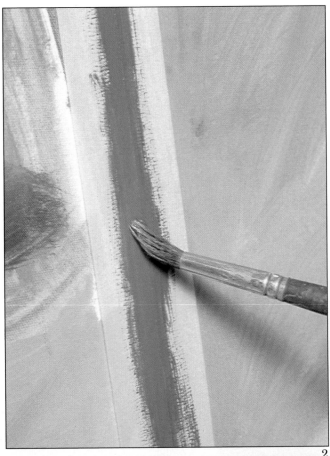

2

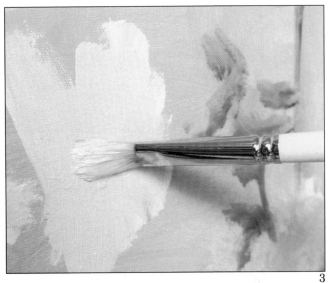

3

LEFT Once the underpainting was complete, the picture was built up with thicker paint, and more colours were introduced. The photograph (ABOVE) **3** shows a thick mixture of yellow and white being used for one of the flagstones over an underlayer of pinkish-brown. Other flagstones were painted in shades of blue and muted grey.

Thick paint is being applied (BELOW LEFT) **4** to define the rim of the pot, and the foliage is being built up (BELOW) **5** with areas of scumbled paint and thick brushstrokes of yellow-green.

4

5

6

MATERIALS USED

- Support: bought,
  ready-primed
  canvas 76.2 ×
  50.8 cm (30 ×
  20 in)
- Brushes: two flat
  hog's-hair,
  numbers 5 and 12,
  one number 12
  soft synthetic
- Colours: titanium
  white, Payne's
  grey, burnt
  umber, raw
  umber, cobalt
  blue, cadmium
  red, Naples
  yellow, sap green,
  chrome green,
  viridian and
  chrome oxide

ABOVE **6** This detail of the
foreground foliage illustrates
the way in which paint and
particular brushes can be
used to create texture. The
leaves here are suggested by
short, curving brushstrokes,
using thick paint over a still-
wet layer beneath it so that
the colour does not go on
totally flat but is modified by
the one beneath. No attempt
has been made to define all
the leaves, and some areas
have been left quite loosely
painted, adding to the
spontaneous and free effect.

RIGHT **7** The artist uses his
fingers to smudge in
highlights.

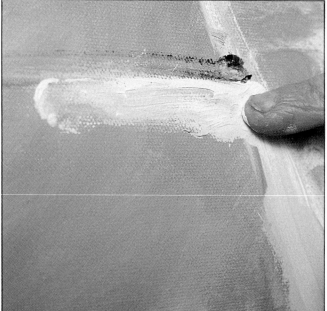

7

SEASCAPE OFF CRETE

THIS painting provides a contrast to that on page 51, as in this case the paint was used thickly on a very coarse-grained type of canvas called scrim. This is too flimsy to be stretched in the conventional way; so it was stuck down on a piece of hardboard with glue size.

The inspiration for the painting came from some photographs taken on holiday in Crete in blustery autumn weather. The painting set out to recapture the look of a harbour in late evening in far from tranquil weather, and the way the paint has been used gives an added drama and immediacy, so that it looks as though it could have actually been painted quickly on the spot. The particular photograph used as a reference is quite dull, but the painter has drawn on his own recollections for the colour scheme and composition.

The composition is a simple one, with the sea, the foreground and the background all being similar wedge shapes, relieved by repeated horizontal lines at irregular intervals. The buildings, little more than suggested shapes treated broadly and boldly, provide interest without in any way detracting from the focal point, which is the sea, shining with the reflected evening light.

Because scrim is such a coarse surface, it absorbs a good deal of the paint, which has to be applied thickly to cover it. Also, the paint covers such a surface unevenly, catching on some parts and sinking into others, effects which have been exploited in this painting to create an interesting, lively paint surface. Other effects have been used too: when painting the sea the artist squeezed white paint on to the support direct from the tube and then used yellow oil pastel in blobs on top of a layer of blue paint. The buildings were defined by drawing on to dry paint with a pencil, and some of the paint in the foreground area was wiped on with a rag. This is an excellent demonstration of the way in which different techniques and media can be combined to good effect. Some people feel inhibited about mixing media, believing that it is not 'proper' painting, but it is a mistake to feel restricted to the contents of your paint box – if you want to mix paint with sand and apply it with your fingers, and it seems to work, then do so.

1

ABOVE **1** Paint was applied thickly with a loaded brush and scrubbed into the surface. The colour used here was a mixture of white and cerulean blue, and the way in which the warm colour of the ground has been allowed to show through in places enhances it, whereas if the ground had been white it might have detracted from the effect of the blue.

BELOW **2** The basic composition of the picture – interlocking wedge shapes – can be seen very clearly at this stage, when the hills in the background have not yet been painted. The sea has been blocked in roughly, with a modified version of the same colour repeated in the sky.

2

3

4

5

6

TOP LEFT **3** This detail shows yellow oil pastel being dabbed into the blue of the sea. This enhances the blue, since blue and yellow are complementary colours, as does the golden colour of the ground showing through.

TOP RIGHT **4** For the foreground, a mixture of black and raw umber was applied with a rag in broad sweeps. Here, too, the golden colour of the ground has been allowed to show through in places, modifying the darker layer of paint.

BELOW LEFT **5** The artist has allowed the colour of the support to show through the blue for the sky by applying the paint quite thinly.

ABOVE **6** In the detail a pencil is being used to redefine the buildings, which had become rather amorphous in shape. The pencil also modifies and darkens the colours beneath, in the same way as would applying a dark glaze to a lighter colour beneath.

7

MATERIALS USED

- Support: scrim-covered hardboard prepared with size but no other ground
- Brushes: number 12 flat only. Paint was also applied with a rag, and a yellow oil pastel was used on top of the paint in places.
- Colours: titanium white, ivory black, cerulean blue, Mars yellow, Naples yellow, burnt sienna, raw sienna, raw umber and ultramarine

ABOVE **7** The details show white paint being squeezed on to the support straight from the tube and then smeared with the fingers to blend it into the surrounding areas. The effect of direct application like this onto a coarse-grained support can clearly be seen in the finished painting (OPPOSITE).

AUTUMN MISTS

THIS painting, done on the spot on a grey autumn day, has a quiet harmony that captures the quality of both the type of landscape and the lighting. The light on days like this tends to have a flattening effect as there is no sunlight to cast shadows and create dramatic tonal contrasts, and distant objects look nearer for this reason – on a bright day this particular landscape would have had a totally different appearance. A grey sky and muted light can, however, provide a subtle but glowing range of colours, which have been fully exploited here; even the background was painted in pure, clear blues.

When painting out of doors, you may be tempted to ignore composition or think it is irrelevant – you are just 'painting what you see', after all. This is not really the case, as composition is always important; indeed you will find you are almost subconsciously composing as soon as you start to put a line on the canvas, by selecting some elements, exaggerating others, placing the horizon in a particular position, and so on. Here the composition is simple but effective, and was established at the outset by a sketchy line drawing. The curves of the path, dividing the foreground into a series of triangular sections, lead the eye to the strong horizontal line at the base of the tall tree, and from this point the main lines are the vertical ones of the trees reaching up to the sky. All the compositional elements are important: the tree on the left, going out of the frame at the top, is balanced by the one on the right, while the gentle diagonal at the base of the right-hand tree breaks up the broad horizontals elsewhere in the painting. An interesting exercise is to block out one part of a picture and note how it alters the whole balance. If, for instance, you block out the right-hand tree with your finger you will see that it results in an unbalanced, uneasy composition, where the eye has 'nowhere to go'.

The painting was done rapidly, the main areas being initially blocked in in shades of ochre and grey to establish the middle tones. Quite a small range of colours was used – one green, one blue, one bright yellow and four browns and ochres as well as white, as this subject did not require a great range. When working out of doors, it is a good idea to restrict your palette in this way, as otherwise you will be tempted to use too many colours, which can often spoil the unity of a painting.

1

LEFT **1** The broad outlines were drawn in with a fine sable brush and cobalt blue paint very much thinned. This type of painting does not require a detailed underdrawing, but it is essential to establish the main elements of the composition.

BELOW **2** As the effect of the painting depends on the relationship of the various broad masses of colour, the artist began to apply colour immediately, working all over the painting and placing the cool and warm middle tones in relation to one another. These, once established, provide a key against which the darker and brighter colours could be assessed.

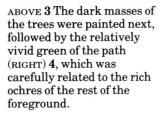

ABOVE **3** The dark masses of the trees were painted next, followed by the relatively vivid green of the path (RIGHT) **4**, which was carefully related to the rich ochres of the rest of the foreground.

3

2

4

5

MATERIALS USED

- Support: fine-grained canvas 76 cm (30 in) square, primed with animal-skin size and an oil ground
- Brushes: numbers 2 to 8 in both flats and rounds, with a number 4 sable for the initial drawing and the final details
- Colours: titanium white, lemon yellow, yellow ochre, burnt sienna, raw umber, alizarin crimson, cobalt blue and viridian

ABOVE **5** The colours of the background were modified and 'cooled' to increase the sense of space by making the background appear to recede.

RIGHT Finally, a small sable brush was used to paint the details of the distant trees, and the area at the base of the right-hand tree was darkened and defined.

GREEK VILLAGE

THIS painting was not done on the spot, but it is the result of much sketching and observation of a particular part of Greece, where the painter frequently spends holidays, and it captures the sun-soaked Mediterranean atmosphere very successfully. A series of drawings was made for the painting, together with colour notes and photographs, so that the composition and colour scheme could be planned and worked out from a wide range of reference material.

The painting shows a view from a window, a subject which often makes an interesting composition as the viewpoint is higher than the usual street-level one and tends to include more varied elements. In this case, the bird's-eye view of the rooftops provides an attractive contrast to the smaller rectangles of window frames and doors, and the straight lines of the buildings are balanced and enhanced by the curves of the trees, foliage-covered walls and the vegetable patch in the foreground, which lead the eye into the picture. The taut diagonals of the two rows of steps give an effect of movement and rhythm to the whole composition, which is full of interest and detail without being in any way fussy – even the small figures and the chairs and tubs on the balcony play a part in the scene, but are never allowed to dominate it. The balance of lights and darks is particularly important in this painting, as the artist wanted to capture the effect of the bright Mediterranean light, which creates strong tonal contrasts.

The painting was completed in one day. The paint was used quite thinly to begin with and built up to a thicker and richer surface as the work progressed (this is the classic oil painting method known as working 'fat over lean'). The quality of the brushstrokes is an integral part of the painting, and has been used in places to create textures and suggest forms, such as in the tree and the vegetable patch in the foreground.

The support was a fine-grained canvas, particularly suitable for a painting with areas of small detail and sharp straight lines, which would be more difficult to achieve on a very coarse canvas.

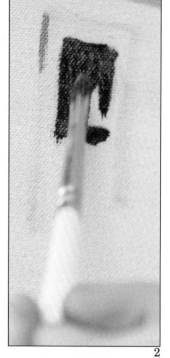

ABOVE **1** An underdrawing was done on the support using a small brush and cobalt blue paint heavily diluted with turpentine. Although the drawing itself was not very detailed, the painting had already been carefully planned, a necessary preliminary for a subject as complex as this one with its many contrasting shapes and tones. The artist then proceeded to block in the mid-tones, using thinned paint. Once these were established they provided a key for the lighter and darker tones. Another artist might have worked in a quite different way, doing a monochrome underpainting or charcoal drawing to establish the lights and darks first.

ABOVE **2** With the mid-tones established, together with the main lines of the drawing, the architectural details could be drawn in with dark paint.

RIGHT **5** The areas of foliage were then developed using viridian and raw umber for the dark tones and lemon yellow and cobalt blue for the lighter ones.

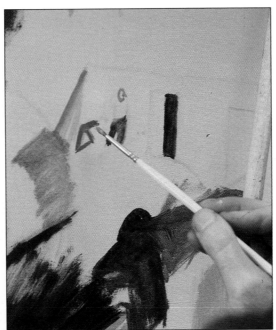

FAR LEFT **3** The artist rests his hand on a mahl stick to steady it while he draws a precise curve. The mahl stick is held in the non-painting hand with the cushioned end resting on a dry part of the canvas, or on the edge of it if the paint is wet. In a painting like this, careful drawing is essential – an inaccurately placed window frame or a crooked roofline would have a jarring effect, and spoil the overall harmony of the picture.

LEFT **4** A small round bristle brush was used to paint in the figures, giving detail without being over-meticulous.

3

4

5

6

MATERIALS USED

- Support: finely woven, ready-primed canvas 91 × 122 cm (36 × 48 in)
- Brushes: a selection of hog's-hair rounds ranging from numbers 6 to 10, with a number 4 sable used for the underdrawing
- Colours: titanium white, lemon yellow, Naples yellow, yellow ochre, burnt sienna, raw umber, cadmium red, alizarin crimson, cobalt blue, ultramarine, viridian and sap green. The painting mediums were linseed oil and turpentine

ABOVE **6** AND RIGHT At this stage, with all the main tones and colours established, the painting has emerged as a complete entity, whereas previously it had been a series of disparate elements. The feeling of warmth in the greys and shadow areas was achieved by mixing alizarin crimson into the cooler colours, while mixtures of white, yellow ochre, Naples yellow and burnt sienna were used for the warm browns and yellows. The colours were then modified and some areas developed and clarified, with the paint applied more thickly, and the final details such as the chairs on the balcony were added.

LANDSCAPE WITH PALM TREES

A PHOTOGRAPH provided the main reference for this painting, and in this case it was quite adequate, as the shapes are all quite bold and clearly defined. However, the photograph is noticeably dull in comparison with the painting, which reflects the artist's interests and ideas in a highly personal way. The paint has been used in a way which creates its own excitement and drama, enhancing the spikiness of the trees in the foreground and the angularity of the cypresses.

One of the most striking features of the painting is the sense of depth and recession which the artist has managed to convey through the use of aerial perspective (see page 31). The mountain in the background is painted in pale shades of grey with rather thin paint, while the foreground has much more tonal contrast, and the paint has been applied very boldly, with vigorous brushstrokes. Another device used to increase the feeling of space was to allow the main vertical shapes, the palm trees, to go out of the frame at the top and bottom of the picture, thus bringing them forward so that they exist on what is usually referred to as the 'picture plane', while the cypresses are clearly further back in space, in the middle distance.

The composition itself has departed from that in the photograph in seemingly minor, but actually vitally important, ways. The uncomfortable central placing of the two trees in the photograph has been changed to place the tall tree slightly further to the right, with the front tree to the left so that it balances the cypresses, while the tree at the far right has been brought just far enough into the picture for it to read as a tree rather than as an anonymous and rather dull shape. The detail of the middle distance has been considerably simplified, and the foliage at the top left given a more definite and pleasing overall shape. When working from photographs, always allow yourself to change the composition in whatever ways you feel will benefit the painting, even if you have taken the photograph specially with a particular painting in mind.

The paint itself has been applied in a way which creates an interesting surface, an important aspect of any painting. A variety of brushes was used to create a range of textural effects; thick paint was drawn into with the handle of a brush and scraped into with a knife (the technique known as *sgraffito*); and paint was flicked on with a painting knife to suggest foliage and the bark of the palm tree in the foreground. The palette itself was limited to only six colours plus white, an unusually small selection which has nevertheless produced a lively and varied colour scheme.

1

2

TOP LEFT **1** A rough pencil drawing was done on the canvas, after which the painting was begun with very diluted paint, each area being developed at the same time. Using paint thinned with turpentine and just a little linseed oil enabled the main shapes to be blocked in quite quickly. At this stage all the main areas had been blocked in and the canvas was completely covered, but the shapes were as yet treated only as broad, flat areas, and the foliage at the top righthand side had not been treated at all.

BELOW LEFT **2** The foliage was added when the paint for the sky was fairly dry, and a painting knife was used to flick on the paint. This gave an effect unlike any that could be achieved with a brush. It needs a sure hand to use a painting knife with confidence.

LEFT **3** The side of the painting knife was used to put on thick paint over a thinner layer below in a way that suggests the texture of the bark of the tree. Techniques such as this give a feeling of drama and excitement to a painting as well as creating areas of decorative texture. The thickly applied paint representing the trunk of the tall tree was drawn into with the handle of a brush (BELOW) **4** to suggest the spiky palm fronds.

3

4

- Support: ready-primed canvas board 76 × 61 cm (30 × 24 in)
- Brushes: bristle numbers 6 to 12 in both flats and rounds together with soft synthetic brushes for the finer details and a medium sized painting knife
- Colours: titanium white, ivory black, yellow ochre, alizarin crimson, raw umber, Prussian blue, Hooker's green, and the painting mediums were linseed oil and turpentine

5

LEFT **5** Paint was smudged on with the fingers and a small piece of rag in places where a soft effect was desired. The foliage was further defined by using a soft brush to work thick paint on top of the still-wet layer below. This is called 'working wet into wet'; the top layer will pick up some of the paint from the layer below, an effect which is exploited deliberately in paintings such as this.

6

LEFT **6** Texture was added to the tall tree and the mountain was defined with cool, pale greys to increase the sense of space (cool colours recede, while warm ones come forward). The cypress trees just in front of the mountain were added, being just suggested with one brushstroke each, working wet into wet so that the green was modified by being allowed to pick up some of the underlying grey.

DERELICT PIER

THIS subject is an ambitious one in which accuracy of drawing is particularly important; so several careful pen-and-ink studies were made before the painting was begun. (Rain came before the one illustrated was completed – hence the splashes.) The main lines of the pier, with its railings, seats, lamp-posts and buildings, were then drawn on to the support with charcoal. Note the diagonal line running through the tops of the lamp-posts, enabling the perspective to be plotted correctly. The drawing was tightened up and emphasized in places with thinned black paint and a small brush, after which the main colour areas were blocked in with grey, green and yellow ochre. The paint was initially used quite thinly, and applied with flat bristle brushes. Patches of the white support were allowed to show through in places, but the paint became thicker as the painting progressed, finally being built up into a rich scumbled surface which is extremely satisfying to the eye.

The composition is based on the relationship of the diagonal and vertical lines, with those of the railings leading in to the strong vertical formed by the outer edge of the building and then up to the opposing diagonal of the eave of the roof, which takes the eye back to the centre again. The curves – of the arches, lamp-posts and seat arms – act as a counterpoint to the taut, angular shapes.

The colour range is quite limited, but the colours nevertheless glow and shimmer with life, partly because of the way the paint has been physically applied and partly because of the way the colours themselves are juxtaposed. The building on the right, for example, could have been treated simply as an area of flat grey, but here rich colour has been introduced, with relatively bright patches of blue and yellow inside the arch, while blues and yellows recur on the front of the building, echoing the greens of the sea and the rich ochres of the pier top. Even the lamp-posts and seat arms have been warmed and enlivened by touches of muted yellow, which occur again in a stronger form in the area at the bottom of the railings, representing the reflected light from the sea.

ABOVE RIGHT **1** The main lines were drawn on to the support with willow charcoal. This was then dusted off and the lines were strengthened with thinned black paint applied with a fine synthetic brush. (RIGHT) **2** The lines of black have been overpainted very little, so that they are still visible as an integral part of the finished work. The artist worked from several sketches, but developed the painting further, so that it is not identical to any of them.

1

2

LEFT **3** AND BELOW **4** The sea was laid in first as a flat area of green, which was then given warmth and a feeling of light and movement by cross-hatching with brushstrokes of burnt sienna, white and red. There is a strong element of perspective in this painting, and the artist has used the railings against the large blocks of colour as a visual device to lead the eye of the viewer straight into the picture. The brushstrokes are very much part of the composition, and have been used in a directional way to strengthen the effect; those on the seat follow and accentuate the form (BOTTOM LEFT) **5** and those on the railings are worked round rather than along the forms. This has also helped to suggest the texture of the old metal.

3

4

5

MATERIALS USED

- Support: smooth side of a piece of hardboard 60 × 75 cm (24 × 30 in), which had been sanded down before priming to remove the shine. Some of the sanding dust was left on the board to provide texture, and it was then primed with white gesso primer
- Brushes: Dalon synthetics, numbers 4 to 11, which the artist liked because they are less soft than nylon and give a good, fine point for detailed work
- Colours: titanium white, yellow ochre, light red, burnt sienna, ultramarine, sap green, cadmium green and lamp black, which is warmer than ivory black and gives deep, rich tones when mixed with ultramarine

ABOVE **6** The brushstrokes on the building are straight, following the vertical plane, and they have not been blended or worked together, so as to leave the paint surface clean and fresh. Although quite bright colours have been introduced here, they have been very carefully related to each other so that no one colour jumps forward or assumes undue importance. This is much more difficult than it looks.

RIGHT The final touches involved more work on the building and the addition of a scumbled texture over the whole painting, heightening the impression of old, crumbling metal.

CHAPTER SIX

INDOOR

SUBJECTS

ALL the paintings on the following pages, whether portraits, figure studies, still-lifes or flower paintings, have one thing in common – they have all been done under conditions which are in the control of the artists themselves. A portrait or still-life can be set up in whatever way you want – you can usually dictate what your model should wear and what the background will consist of, and you can decide what objects you want in your still-life or flower painting.

All this can be an advantage, as it means you need not feel rushed, but it can also be a disadvantage, as that very sense or urgency you feel when confronted with a subject that must be captured quickly can often produce a more interesting painting. One way of artificially creating this sense of urgency, and thus not allowing yourself to fall prey to the temptation of niggling away at a picture, is to set yourself a time limit. Take as long as you like over arranging and lighting a still-life or doing preliminary drawings for a portrait, but when you start the painting, decide that you will complete it in one or two sessions.

The only drawing for the portrait consisted of a few lines and outlines made with a number 3 bristle brush and thinned paint, **1** after which yellows, blues and warm red-browns were laid on, to be modified and defined later **2**. A rag was used to wipe off some paint from the forehead, cheeks and chin, **3** thus lightening the highlight areas. It was also used to smooth the previously roughly-applied paint in the background, removing some of the excess. **4** and **5** Shadows and highlights were built up in the face and hair,

PORTRAIT OF A MAN WITH A BEARD

THIS portrait was done quite quickly, in only two sessions, and has a fresh and spontaneous quality. Portraits often have to be completed in less time than the painter would perhaps consider ideal, since few sitters have either the time or the inclination to sit in one position for long periods of time. This particular portrait was actually done mainly from the photograph, which was freely adapted to convey the artist's own impression of the subject's colouring and character rather than being used as a 'copy' to be re-produced in paint. He could, of course, have taken much longer over the painting since he was not work-ing from a live model, but he preferred to simulate the conditions of working from life in order to avoid an overworked, tired painting. It is often a good idea to set yourself a time limit in this way, both with portraits and landscapes, and to try to rely on your original impressions of a face or scene rather than peering at a photograph and trying to find the exact shade or line you seem to see in it.

the paint being blended with a bristle brush and short, dabbing strokes. Because the painting was done on hardboard, which is not very absorbent, only turpentine was used as the medium at this stage, as the addition of oil would have made the paint too sloppy and caused it to dry too slowly.
6 Even so, by the sixth stage the paint had now become too thick and wet to work on satisfactorily, so the whole surface was blotted with newspaper, which removed the excess layer while still leaving a quite distinct image.

1

2

3

4

5

6

RIGHT **7** A piece of newspaper was applied, pressed lightly and lifted off, to remove some of the surplus paint. Blotting paper or towelling can also be used for this purpose.

7

BELOW **8** A rag was used to clean up the area on the face where the paint had become too thick.

8

The painting was begun with an underdrawing in neutral browns and blues, using thinned paint, after which layers of thicker paint were built up. The facial features were left quite undefined in the early stages, emerging only gradually from the broadly treated planes of the face, and the scarf was added later almost as an afterthought. All areas of the painting were worked on at the same time, the whole canvas being covered almost immediately, so that the relationship of the tones and colours could be assessed, balanced and altered where necessary. When the head was reasonably complete the artist decided to lighten the colours of the background, which also gave him an opportunity to correct and redefine the outline of the face. The tones and colours of the flesh were then adjusted in relation to the new background, and the relatively bright colours of the scarf blocked in to balance them. In oil painting, almost any such alterations can be made, but it is easier to work light over dark because white is the most opaque colour. If the painting had started with a light background, an attempt to change it to a dark one would probably have been unsatisfactory.

Because the painting was done quickly, there was no time to allow the paint to dry between stages, so a rag or a piece of newspaper was used from time to time to lightly blot the surface, removing the excess paint. A rag was also used to spread the paint in the background areas and to lighten the highlights in the early stages. Such techniques are particularly useful when working on a non-absorbent surface such as hardboard, which can easily become so overloaded with paint that successive layers stir it up and muddy it.

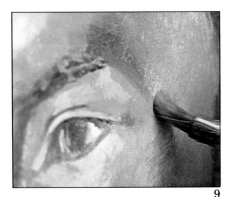

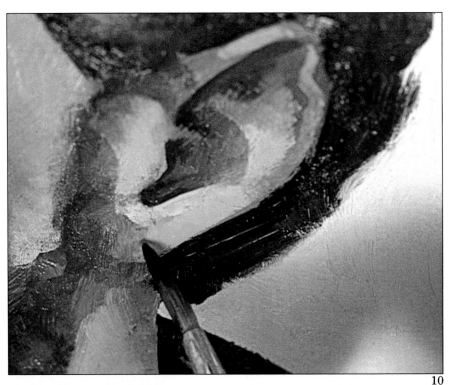

ABOVE **9** and RIGHT **10** Using a small brush, the artist begins to work on the more detailed areas of the painting to define the hitherto vague facial features.

MATERIALS USED

- Support: primed hardboard 45 × 30 cm (18 × 12 in)
- Brushes: number 3 flat bristle and a number 5 round sable for the fine details
- Colours: titanium white, ivory black, cadmium yellow, yellow ochre, vandyke brown, cobalt blue, ultramarine, chrome oxide and vermilion, and the painting mediums were turpentine and linseed oil

ABOVE **11** and **12** When the painting was almost finished it became clear to the artist that it needed to be lightened in tone; so he overpainted the background, taking the opportunity to correct the outline of the face at the same time, and then adjusted the colours and tones of the flesh, blending the paint with light brushstrokes. He then altered the righthand side of the background again, so that from being the darker side it became the lighter one – almost white. The scarf, seen in the finished painting, was not originally planned as part of the composition, but the heightened tones and colours seemed to need a balance, and it was added as a final touch. This portrait provides an excellent example of the way in which oil paintings can be altered again and again without loss of quality.

OPPOSITE Earlier stages involved covering the face with a reddish glaze, giving a warmth and glow to the flesh. The effect of this is clearly visible in both the detail of the brow area and in the finished painting.

ANITA IN MINIATURE

T HIS is a particularly interesting portrait because, although the treatment is bold and free, with clearly visible brushstrokes, the painting is very small, almost the same size as reproduced here. As this artist usually works on quite a large scale, producing a portrait as small as this presented something of a challenge, but she has met it with considerable success. It can be rather disturbing suddenly to change scale from a size which seems natural to one which does not, and this sometimes results in a different style being used, which the painter is not really at home with. In this case, however, the artist has managed to reduce the scale without detriment to her normal colourful and bold style.

As the portrait had to be completed quickly, a piece of cardboard was used for mixing the colours instead of the conventional palette, which had the effect of absorbing some of the oil and letting the paint dry more rapidly. Turpentine, used as the medium, also speeded the drying and provided a matt surface, which this artist prefers. Sable brushes were used in place of the more usual bristle ones in order to apply the paint carefully in small blocks, which were then blended lightly into one another. The colours have been considerably heightened and exaggerated, with the background appearing as an area of clear, bright blue and the face itself composed of separate, though related, patches of pure colour. This type of colour is known as high key, as opposed to low key, where all the colours are more sombre. An artist sometimes makes a deliberate choice to paint a particular subject in a particular key, but often it is more or less an instinctive thing. Some artists always paint in a low key, even when the subject is colourful, and others automatically heighten all the colours. The brightness of this painting was deliberate, and is enhanced by the use of a pure white support, with no underpainting; the white is reflected back through the paint, giving the colours extra sparkle and translucency.

1

ABOVE **1** A careful pencil drawing was done first, and was particularly necessary in this case, since for such a small painting inaccurate drawing or a clumsy placing of the head in relation to the background could be disastrous. As you can see by comparing the finished painting with the photograph, the area of the pink blouse has been reduced to just two small triangles; these balance the bright colours of the flesh and lips. The area of background is greater on the left side of the face than the right, thus avoiding monotony. Even in a head-only portrait composition this is important and should be planned at the outset.

OPPOSITE **2** The pencil lines, which were quite dense, were rubbed down lightly with a rag before the paint was applied, to prevent the graphite dust mixing with and muddying the colours.

The first flesh tints, mixed from a wide variety of pure colours, were then applied, and the planes of light and shade began to emerge. Note how the strip of cool, pale colour down the side of the face – the reflected light visible in the photograph – prevents the similar tones of the background and the shadow area of the face from merging together. The area of blue was blocked in at an early stage so that the flesh tones could be related to the colour of the background, and the artist put dabs of colour and tone on to the unpainted side of the face to help offset the effect of the glaring white canvas.

2

RIGHT **3** AND BELOW **4** The areas of pale flesh tones, mainly mixed from red, yellow ochre and white are being applied to the neck and taken right up to the background. The paint was used fairly thickly so that it was opaque enough to cover the blue and give a clearly defined line. The bright pink area around the eye, applied with a small brush, reflects the bright rose of the blouse, as does the shadow under the chin.

RIGHT **5** The only parts left to be painted at this stage were the lips, the headscarf and the hair over the forehead, with the hair being treated quite broadly and with little detail.

3

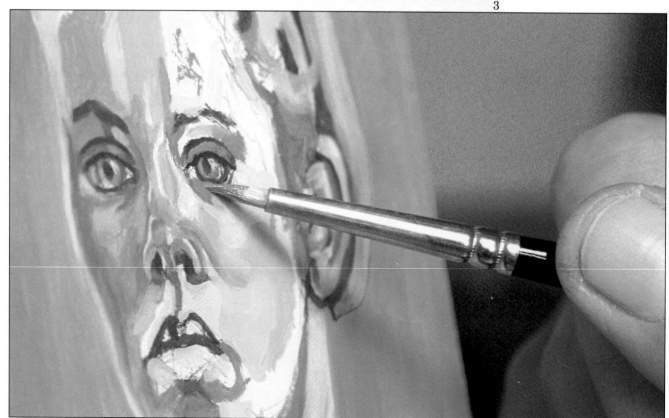

4

5

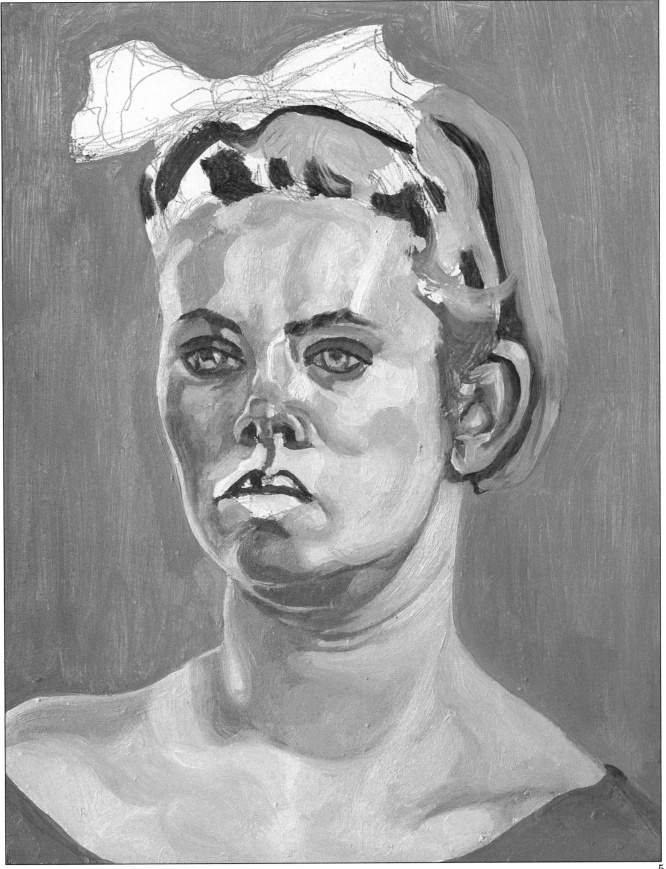

RIGHT **6** The lips were painted next, and then the patterned scarf, in which each colour was carefully related to those in the face itself. When painting in such a high colour key, much care and thought is needed to relate the colours to each other, otherwise there will be unpleasant discords. The hair was then modified in colour so as to emphasize the bright colours of the scarf, and the fringe was defined with free, bold brushstrokes.

OPPOSITE Note how the whole portrait is 'lifted' by the patterned scarf and red lips – all the colours suddenly appear brighter and the entire image is crisper.

MATERIALS USED

- Support: primed hardboard about 15.5 × 12.5 cm (6 × 5 in)
- Brushes: round sable numbers 2, 3, 5 and 8, and the paint was thinned with turpentine alone
- Colours: titanium white, yellow ochre, Naples yellow, cadmium yellow, cadmium red, alizarin crimson, Rowney rose, violet, cobalt blue, ultramarine, cerulean blue and terre verte

6

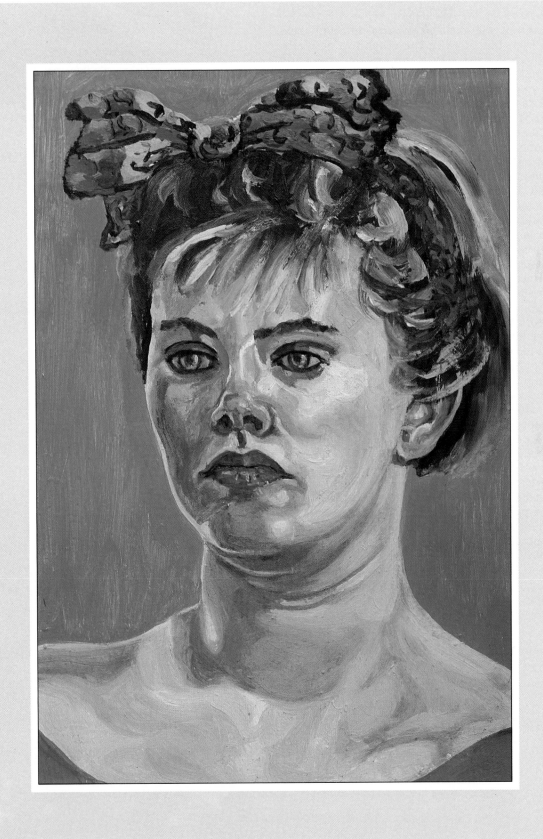

THIS painting was done in a quite different technique from that used in the other two portraits; the paint here is used very thinly, so that the early stages resemble a watercolour. The colours are also much less vivid, the emphasis being on the contrasts of lights and darks.

A profile is a difficult subject, and profile portraits are not often done, the three-quarter view being the preferred one. This is partly because a profile can look rather boring and unsubtle, and partly because, of course, it does not allow the eyes, the usual focal point of a portrait, to show. Here, an interesting composition has been made by placing the head to one side so that the back and top are cut off, with the line of the hair creating a bold curve to break up what would otherwise have been a stark vertical at the edge of the canvas. The artist has given the space around the head an importance of its own by painting it flat and allowing it to occupy almost as much of the total picture area as the profile itself. The picture can thus be seen as two interlocking areas (this is particularly noticeable if you look at it upside down). This concept is sometimes called 'negative space', and can form a very important part in a composition, the 'negative' space being used to balance the 'positive' image.

The luminous quality of the shadow area of the face has been achieved by *glazing,* a technique of applying thinned paint in layers, one over the other. Glazing is a slow process, as each layer must be dry before the next is applied, but it is a particularly suitable technique for painting flesh, and was much used by the early painters in oil, such as Jan van Eyck. In this case, linseed oil with a very little turpentine was used to thin the paint for the glazes, but linseed oil is not actually the best medium for this technique. A special alkyd medium called Liquin is now manufactured and sold specifically for the purpose; it dries fast and binds the pigment so that the glaze, however thin, will stay where it is put, instead of dribbling down the surface of the support, as can happen with linseed oil.

2

3

LEFT **1** A simple but accurate
line drawing was done of the
profile, including indications
of the shapes of the
highlights on the cheekbone,
nose and chin. The
background area was then
blocked in with a thin wash
of grey paint applied with a
number 4 flat bristle brush,
and a wash of burnt umber
was used for the shadow
under the brow.

TOP RIGHT **2** The warm tones
were established next, using
a mixture of yellow ochre and
white for the hair, and burnt
umber, cadmium red and
titanium white for the face.

ABOVE **3** The shadows around
the eyes were painted with a
smaller bristle brush, a
number 2, each separate
block of colour and tone
being carefully delineated.

1

BELOW **4** The skin tones were developed more fully by applying diluted paint in very thin glazes which allow light to bounce off the canvas and back through the colours. This produces a luminous glow which cannot be achieved with opaque paint. Glazes can also be laid over a layer of thick, impasted paint to modify the underlying colour, a method used by both Rembrandt and Turner. Here, however, all the layers are thin; in the detail the texture of the canvas is quite clearly visible through the paint.

OPPOSITE As a final touch, fine strands of hair were added above the forehead and beside the cheek and chin, using a very fine brush and a mixture of titanium white and yellow ochre. Note how these few lines 'lift' the whole portrait, hinting at the quality of the fine hair and breaking up the large area of background while allowing it still to exist as a definite shape.

MATERIALS USED

- ● Support: small, fine-grained canvas board bought ready-primed, 37.5 × 30 cm (15 × 12 in)
- ● Brushes: flat bristle, with a small sable for the fine lines
- ● Colours: titanium white, ivory black, burnt sienna, burnt umber, yellow ochre, cadmium red medium, scarlet lake and ultramarine. The mediums were linseed oil and turpentine, with a much higher proportion of linseed oil used for the glazing

4

1

2

3

NUDE AND SUNLIGHT

IGURE painting, like portraiture, presents a great many problems, not the least being that of getting the drawing right. When faced with a complex subject such as this, you will find your task much easier if you make the most important decisions *before* you start work. First, decide which aspect of the subject you are actually interested in and then how you intend to treat it. Some artists will be most concerned with attempting to convey the sheer beauty of the human body and the marvellous and varied colours of flesh and hair, while others will be interested in the pattern that might be created by a figure against a background. Another artist might not be concerned with either colour or pattern, and will aim at conveying the dynamic and sculptural qualities of the body, and the way the various planes and shapes relate to one another. Part of this decision will, of course, depend on the model. Some artists' models are beautiful, and cry out to be painted simply as lovely natural forms, while others are less conventionally beautiful but are interesting to a painter in more subtle ways.

This painting shows one particular approach to the subject; here the artist's main interest was not in the body as such, or the colours of the flesh, but in the interplay of shapes and the relationship of lights and darks. While being quite distinctly a 'figure painting', it is quite abstract in feeling, with the figure seen as just one element in the composition. The shadows – both that cast by the figure on the background and that cast on the figure by the window bars – have been given considerable importance, as have the shapes in the background. Another artist, whose preoccupations were different, might have played down these elements, or even excluded some of them, softening the shadows and painting the background as an area of space.

The painting was begun with a careful drawing in pencil, in which the figure was drawn in outline. This is not a method recommended for a beginner, as a drawing such as this, although it looks simple, is the result of years of practice and observation. But a good underdrawing in pencil, charcoal or thinned paint is important in a complicated subject, as without it you will find yourself having to make endless corrections,

ABOVE LEFT **1** A careful drawing was made with a sharp HB pencil, after which the shadow areas and outlines were strengthened with thinned black paint applied with a small brush. It is important to start with a good underdrawing or underpainting to establish the composition to your satisfaction. At this stage, you need to have a firm idea about how much of the figure you want to show, how it should be placed in relation to the background, and so on. It can also be helpful to make some small thumbnail sketches first, before you start to draw on the canvas, as this is often the best way of working out a composition. **2** As the prime concern of the artist was the relationship of light and dark shapes, he painted in the dark areas first so that they provided a 'key' for the rest of the painting, leaving the lighter and brighter areas white at this stage. **3** The shadow areas across the body were painted (with burnt sienna) before the flesh was blocked in, and all the other areas were then related to these.

which may ruin the composition you were aiming at as well as giving you a clogged and overworked paint surface.

The dark side of the figure was then outlined more distinctly with black paint and a small brush, after which the shadow across the body was painted carefully with burnt sienna. The flesh tones were related to this before the red-brown background, related in turn to the flesh tones, was blocked in. Each area of the painting was worked on more or less separately, the yellow patch of sunlight and the bright red patch in the foreground being added at a late stage. This artist had a very accurate idea of how the finished painting would look and so the method has been successful, but an inexperienced painter would find it hard to work in this way, as it would be difficult to assess the colour of the flesh, and the degree of tonal contrast within the body area, against the harsh white of the background.

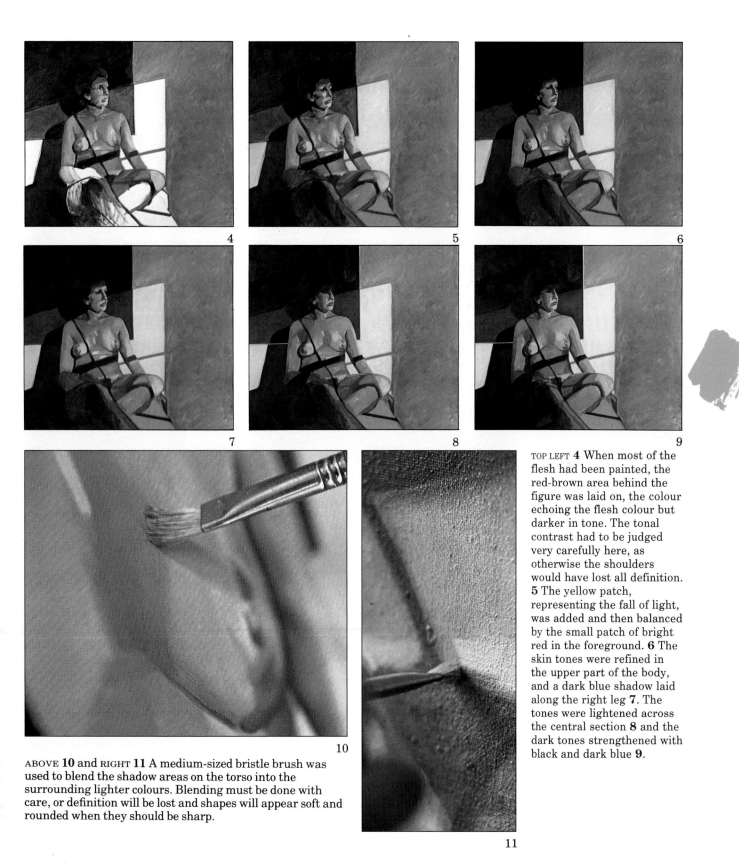

TOP LEFT **4** When most of the flesh had been painted, the red-brown area behind the figure was laid on, the colour echoing the flesh colour but darker in tone. The tonal contrast had to be judged very carefully here, as otherwise the shoulders would have lost all definition. **5** The yellow patch, representing the fall of light, was added and then balanced by the small patch of bright red in the foreground. **6** The skin tones were refined in the upper part of the body, and a dark blue shadow laid along the right leg **7**. The tones were lightened across the central section **8** and the dark tones strengthened with black and dark blue **9**.

ABOVE **10** and RIGHT **11** A medium-sized bristle brush was used to blend the shadow areas on the torso into the surrounding lighter colours. Blending must be done with care, or definition will be lost and shapes will appear soft and rounded when they should be sharp.

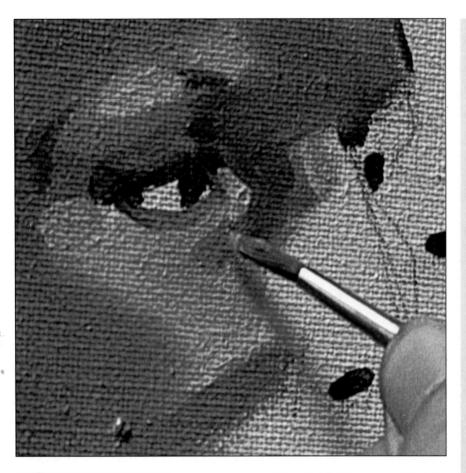

MATERIALS USED

- ● Support: cotton duck, stretched and primed, 90 × 76 cm (36 × 20 in)
- ● Brushes: two number 6 bristle flats, a number 6 round sable and a 2.5-cm (1-in) housepainter's brush for the background areas
- ● Colours: ivory black, titanium white, burnt sienna, raw sienna, raw umber, burnt umber, cadmium yellow, yellow ochre, ultramarine and vermilion. The medium was turpentine alone

ABOVE AND RIGHT The highlight areas and facial details were painted with a fine sable brush and a mid- tone was blended between the shadow and highlight areas. Facial details should be left to a late stage in a figure painting, when you are quite sure no alterations have to be made to the drawing and composition.

DIANA

THIS full-length portrait, or 'clothed figure study', was done partly from life and partly from the photograph. A comparison of the finished painting with the photograph is particularly interesting in this case as it shows how much the artist has simplified the subject in order to deal with what he personally found interesting – the figure itself and the richly glowing blues, violets and orangey-browns. Another artist painting the same subject might have treated it in a quite different way, perhaps including the view through the window, the pattern on the sitter's blouse, and the details on the cupboard, thus making a much busier composition, but here all the emphasis is on the figure itself, with the background areas treated very sketchily so that they do not compete with the main image.

Colour is the dominant aspect of this painting, and the artist has started to place the colours immediately, with only the minimum of underdrawing, using thinned paint in shades of violet and cobalt blue. With the vivid violet of the blouse established, the canvas was then completely covered with thin paint, the colour of the background being more or less that which appears in the finished painting. The background paint was left thin, but the figure itself was built up in thicker paint, and in places the *sgraffito* technique – drawing or scratching into the paint with a knife or brush handle – was used to remove paint from the highlight areas, allowing the white ground to show through.

The composition is a simple one, as befits the subject, with the figure itself placed centrally but made to appear less symmetrical by the placing of the unequal shapes on left and right – the window and cupboard. The image has been given movement and interest by the diagonals formed by the bottom of the window frame, the skirting board and the top and bottom of the cupboard, the latter two leading the eye in to the figure. The angles literally point to the figure so that its central position, which might have resulted in an unfocused or flat painting, is quite acceptable. The bottom corner of the window and the top corner of the cupboard form a triangle with the light reflected from the top of the jeans, providing depth. If the background had been on a flat plane with the skirting board as a horizontal the effect might have been monotonous.

1

2

FAR LEFT **1** The artist began to lay the colour on immediately, using paint very much diluted with turpentine so that it would dry quickly. Marking in the vertical and horizontal lines for the cupboard and background helped him to position the figure correctly.

LEFT **2** As soon as the whole canvas was covered with paint the artist began to work on the highlights to define and sharpen the forms.

RIGHT **3** Here a painting knife is being used to scrape back to the white surface of the canvas.

BELOW RIGHT **4** The arm has now been more fully modelled, with a dark line of shadow down the outside, and a brush handle is being used to draw into it. Some of the purple colour of the blouse has been repeated on the inside of the arm and then scraped away, leaving just enough to suggest the reflected colour in the shadow.

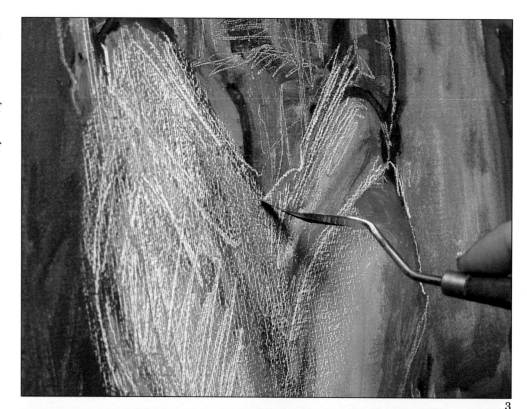

3

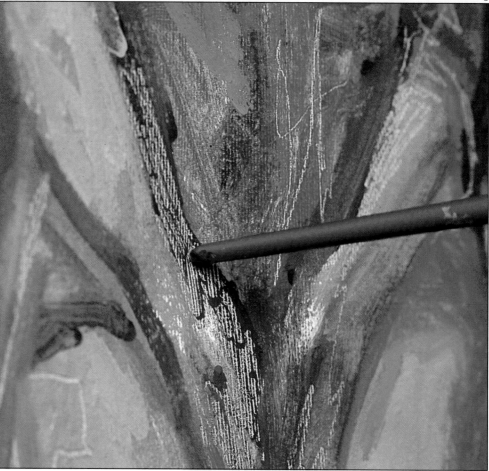

4

LEFT **5** The colour of the blouse and jeans is vitally important to this painting, and the artist has chosen to simplify by ignoring the pattern on the blouse (visible in the photograph) so that it stands as an area of vibrant blue. However, it was not applied as just one colour; mid and dark purple were used for the shadow areas and bright blue for the highlights.

BELOW LEFT **6** Shadows nearly always have a colour of their own rather than being simply a darker shade of the highlight colour.

5

6

RIGHT **7** The face, like the clothing, has been built up in thick paint, freely but carefully applied so that the features are distinct but not over-meticulous. Little blending has been done, but because the artist is working wet into wet the colours are modified by the process of laying one on top of another. The line of blue on the right, representing the reflection from the blouse, has been left quite distinct.

OPPOSITE The finished painting shows how the figure has been given solidity by the use of thick paint and strong tonal contrasts, while the background has been left as areas of quite thin and transparent paint. Although there is little detail in the background, it is not flat and uninteresting; different colours have been used to echo and harmonize with those of the figure itself.

MATERIALS USED

- Support: bought, ready-primed canvas 61 × 46 cm (24 × 18 in)
- Brushes: a selection of bristle and synthetic, a flat bristle being used for the background and small, round synthetics for the face and details of the clothing
- Colours: titanium white, cobalt blue, cerulean blue, cobalt violet, light red, alizarin crimson, yellow ochre, burnt sienna and raw umber. No medium was used except in the early stages, where the paint was thinned with turpentine

7

TEA-CADDY ON A WINDOW SILL

THIS small, quietly harmonious painting, with its limited range of colours and simple subject, provides a contrast with the one on page 112, where the approach is quite different. It also illustrates the way in which colour and composition can be used quite deliberately to create mood: here there are no jarring compositional elements and no bright or discordant colours, but the effect is far from dull – just pleasantly peaceful.

Most people have one or two items about their homes that seem to suggest an idea for a painting, and in this case the artist was attracted to the swelling curves of the pot and its decorative motif. In order to highlight these qualities, he chose to make the composition a geometric one, in which the horizontals and verticals of the window frame and shutter act as a foil for the curved and rounded shapes. The composition is very carefully balanced, with the strip of blue-grey in the foreground just slightly narrower than the window sill above, and the rectangle on the right large enough to be 'read' as the view through the window but not so large as to dominate the painting. The verticals of the window frame have been carefully planned so that they do not interfere with the dominant shapes of the pot and bowl, and the slanting shadows on the left, which appear in the photograph as very distinct areas of tone, are merely hinted at by a very slightly darker colour at the top left.

The paint has been applied very carefully and meticulously, with sable brushes used to build up thin layers, and the support, a fine-grained canvas, was chosen as particularly suitable for this kind of painting. For a picture like this it is important that the straight lines should really be straight – an accidentally slanting vertical line, for example, would provide just the jarring element the artist has been at pains to avoid – so masking tape was used to aid the process. At one time such techniques were considered rather 'mechanical', and frowned upon, but it is extremely difficult to draw a straight line freehand, let alone paint one with a brush, and there is no reason why masking tape or rulers should not be used.

The range of colours used was deliberately very small – just two blues, a green, grey, black and yellow. It can be a useful discipline to limit your colours in this way, choosing just one or two colours and their complementaries (blue and yellow, as here, or red and green) plus greys and browns. It may cut down your choices, but this can also be an advantage as you will have fewer to make, and you may find that your painting achieves a harmony and unity that it might not have had with a whole range of colours at your disposal. It will also teach you far more about mixing colours than reading a whole book on the subject.

1

2

TOP **1** AND ABOVE **2** As the composition is so simple, no underdrawing was necessary. Instead, the main elements were quickly blocked in, using thin paint and a sable brush, in more or less the colours that appear in the finished painting.

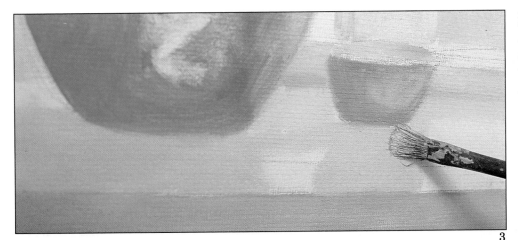

3

4

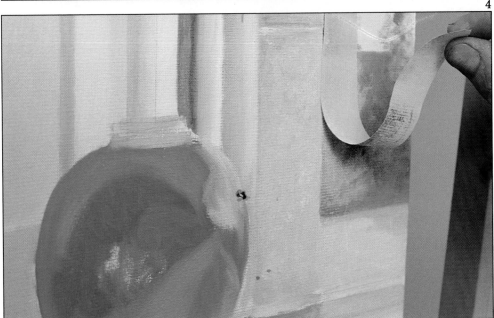

5

LEFT **3** At this stage a bristle brush was used, as the paint was rather thicker (though still relatively thin). The blue of the pot was built up using a mixture of ultramarine and white, with white and Payne's grey used for the window sill. Payne's grey is a useful and versatile colour, with a slight mauvish tinge. Here it appears quite warm in relation to the deep blue. A mixture of black and white would have given a much less 'alive' quality.

LEFT **4** Masking tape was applied to the line which separates the edge of the window frame from the little rectangle of landscape beyond. This allowed the paint to be applied quite freely on the window-frame area.

BELOW LEFT **5** The tape was then lifted off, leaving a clean, straight edge. To use this method successfully the paint must be quite thin and at least semi-dry; otherwise the tape, when lifted off, will take the top layer of paint with it.

RIGHT **6** AND BELOW RIGHT **7**
At this stage, several thin
layers of paint had been built
up one over the other, but
the details, which give a crisp
definition to the finished
painting, had not been
added. In the detail (RIGHT) a
small sable brush is being
used to paint the fine lines
and small cracks at the
bottom of the shutter. If you
look at the finished painting
you will see that this delicate
diagonal line is actually vital
to the composition, leading
the eye to the pot and bowl,
which are the focal points.

OPPOSITE The brickwork was
painted in a mixture of
Payne's grey, yellow ochre
and white, with viridian and
white used for the mini-
landscape through the
window. Great care must be
taken with an area such as
this; if the tonal contrast
were too great or the colours
too bright the landscape
would 'jump' forward,
assuming too much visual
importance and conflicting
with the foreground.
Viridian, being a cool, rather
blue green, is useful for
receding backgrounds.

6

MATERIALS USED

- ● Support: small,
  ready-primed,
  fine-grained
  canvas only 30.5
  × 25.4 cm (12 ×
  10 in)
- ● Brushes: small
  sable and a
  number 8 round
  bristle
- ● Colours: titanium
  white, ivory
  black, Payne's
  grey, yellow
  ochre, cadmium
  yellow pale,
  viridian,
  ultramarine and
  Prussian blue

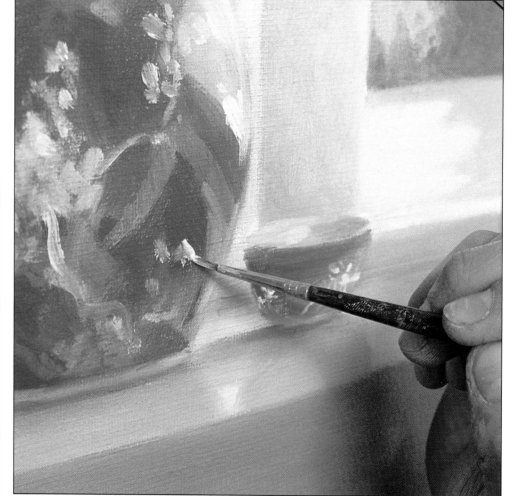

7

STILL-LIFE WITH WATERMELON

THIS still-life, while very different from the one shown on page 105 in its use of thick paint and bright colours, has a rather similar atmosphere of simple, quiet harmony. One of the most difficult aspects of still-life painting is deciding on the initial arrangement; it is only too easy to buy up a green-grocer's entire stock and then find yourself unable to arrive at a satisfactory way of arranging the different elements, or to rush around the house collecting bowls, plates and vases which, when placed together, don't seem to add up to anything you want to paint. Here, as can be seen in the photograph, the artist has chosen a simple arrangement, but one in which the shapes are balanced very carefully.

The composition of the painting is based on a triangle with the point at the top left, and the circular shapes of the plate and half melon intersecting at different angles. The smaller piece of melon echoes the triangle, while the strawberries in the foreground both break up the area of white space and give a feeling of solidity by establishing the plane on which they rest. If you mask them out with your finger you can see how drastically the composition would be weakened and how the main elements would then appear to float in space. The artist has chosen to ignore the line created by the back edge of the table, treating the table top and background as a flat area of 'negative space'; treating the table and wall as separate planes would have detracted from the composition and reduced the importance of the main shapes, which appear almost as though 'carved out' of the space.

A variety of painting techniques has been used to create an interesting paint surface, the first step being a coloured underpainting in very washy paint, after which areas were built up and defined in much thicker paint. The watermelon was given texture by spattering paint on to the surface from a stiff-haired brush; a pencil was used to draw into the fruit; and the white background is very slightly textured with just-visible brushstrokes.

RIGHT **1** A faint underdrawing was done with pencil to position the main elements of the composition, which were then blocked in with heavily-diluted paint.

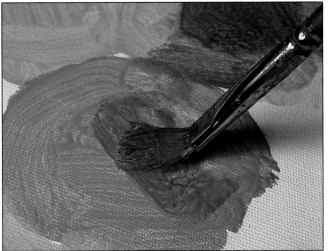

2

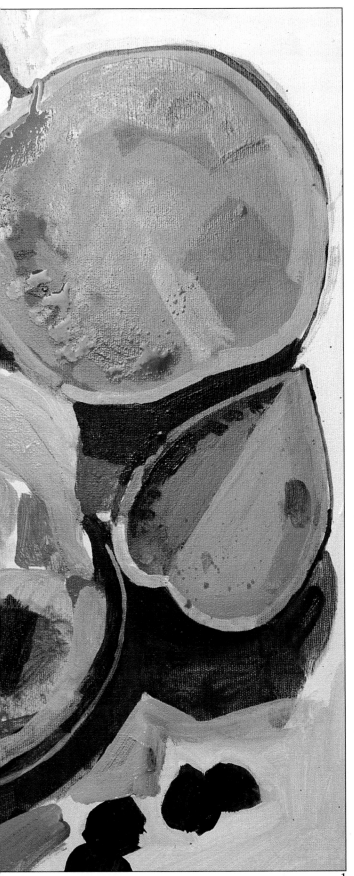

3

1

TOP RIGHT **2** AND ABOVE **3** As soon as the underpainting was dry the artist began to define the separate pieces of fruit, building up the highlights in thick, juicy paint.

4

The artist then drew into the dry paint with a pencil, OPPOSITE **4** a technique which has a dual function in this case as it gives texture and visual interest to the fruit as well as taking down the tones without the necessity for overpainting.

5

LEFT **5** Until now the strawberries had been left as just bold brushstrokes of dark red, but here the artist has given them shape and form, painting the highlights in a light pink and the leaves and stems in bright green.

BELOW **6** The final touch was to modify the shapes by working back into them with white paint and to paint the shadows in blue-grey, clearly outlined on the white background and establishing the plane of the table top.

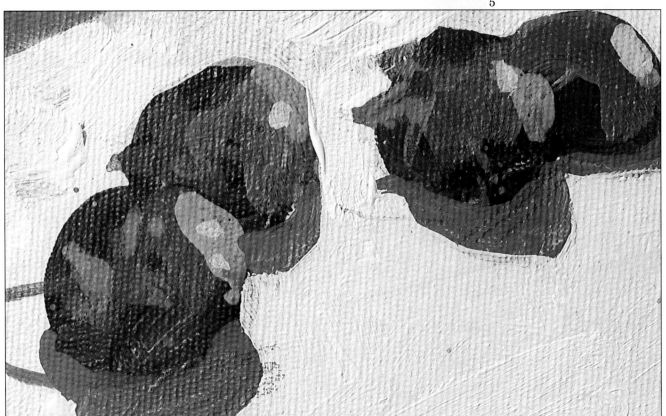

6

RIGHT **7** The watermelon required special treatment, as the texture is an important element of the painting. The artist has chosen a technique he frequently uses – spattering paint from a stiff-haired brush (a toothbrush is often used for this purpose). In order not to splash paint on the rest of the painting he has cut a mask from newspaper, leaving exposed only those areas to be textured. Two tones were used for the spattering, one lighter and one darker than the mid-tone of the underpainting, the paler one echoing the highlights on the strawberries.

BELOW RIGHT **8** The tones and colours were chosen with great care as they had to be light or dark enough to show up, but not so sharply contrasting as to 'jump' off the surface.

7

OPPOSITE In the finished painting the pencil drawing is still just visible on the banana and the apple, and the same technique has been used on the smaller piece of watermelon and on small areas of the shadow under it and the plate. It is touches such as these that give a painting that special 'something', creating extra interest and liveliness; but they should never be allowed to become too important – special techniques are tools, not ends in themselves.

MATERIALS USED

- ● Support: bought, ready-primed canvas board 51 × 40 cm (20 × 16 in)
- ● Brushes: number 12 white bristle and a number 4 hog's hair, with a 2.5-cm (1-in) housepainting brush used for the spattering
- ● Colours: titanium white, yellow ochre, vermilion, cadmium red, cadmium yellow, sap green, cobalt blue and Payne's grey, a range consisting almost entirely of good, strong primaries

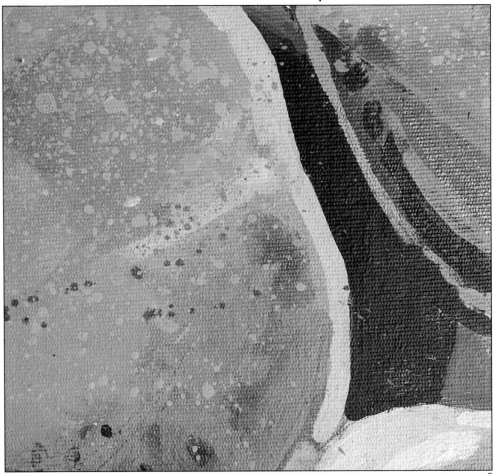

8

FLOWERS ON A WINDOW SILL

ALTHOUGH you would not think it from looking at the painting, this is actually a very difficult subject, presenting a good many problems. The main one is how to deal with the picture planes – the foreground and the space beyond it – in such a way as to create a feeling of space and recession while still retaining the unity of composition which is the hallmark of a successful painting. If the background is allowed to recede too much it will run the risk of becoming dull, but if it comes forward too much it will overwhelm the foreground. The foreground itself has to be given much thought too; otherwise the vase of flowers, which is the focal point, could assume too little importance, and not be strong enough to balance the landscape beyond. Here the artist has solved all the problems very cleverly; the foreground has been given extra importance and interest by the inclusion of the window blind and curtain on one side and the top of a chair on the other, so that an interesting composition exists even without the buildings in the background. The hill village and mountains beyond have been allowed to recede just a little so that they read as a separate and more distant picture plane, but they are still very definitely part of the painting, a landscape in themselves, neatly framed by the verticals of the window. The artist has been lucky, as the hilly terrain has provided a landscape that fits the window; a flatter view would have necessitated a quite different treatment in terms of composition.

The colours used for the landscape echo the deep blues of the vase and cushion, but are slightly nearer one another in tone so that they do not come forward and fight with the foreground. As he worked, the artist had frequently to half-close his eyes, which makes it easier to assess tonal contrasts, and to make small adjustments. Although the colours are vivid and the tonal contrasts bold, the paint itself has been used fairly thinly, in a technique akin to that of watercolour, with small areas of unpainted white canvas left showing in the finished picture. This has given the painting a fresh, sparkling appearance, unlike that achieved by areas of applied white (though there are such areas too). This lively, spontaneous effect is enhanced by the quite rough and sketchy treatment of the window frame and sill, and it is interesting to compare this with the painting on pages 102 to 105, in which the window frame has been treated in a very much more detailed and deliberate fashion. These two paintings, indeed, illustrate very well the radically different ways in which two artists will approach a similar subject.

1

2

TOP **1** This is a complex subject, in which the correct placing of the verticals and horizontals is just as important as the bowl of flowers and the chair top; so a preliminary pencil drawing was made on the canvas to position all the elements in relation to each other. The main shapes were then blocked in in thin colour, the window frame being laid down first, with the bowl and chair painted over the resulting grid. This simple device of overlapping also serves to create depth. At this stage the background has been left as an undefined area of grey-blue in a mid-tone which will act as a key for the more specific tones and colours to be added later. The dark greens of the leaves (ABOVE) **2** provide the key for the darker tones of the foreground.

3

4

LEFT **3** Once the tones of the foreground were established, the artist began to work on the buildings in the landscape, carefully relating the shapes and colours to those in the foreground.

Here yellow ochre is being applied thinly to the roofs, and the row of cypress trees has already been painted, echoing and balancing the leaves on the flowers.

5

ABOVE **4** AND RIGHT **5** Now the artist works on the flowers, deepening the greens, heightening the reds and yellows, and at the same time deepening the blue of the vase. Small areas of the white canvas have been left unpainted, giving a sparkling effect to the leaves and flowers.

RIGHT **6** This detail of the flowers and leaves against the background buildings shows the way the greater tonal contrasts make the flowers stand out just enough to be read as being on a nearer plane. White paint has been applied to the tops of the flowers where they catch the light.

OPPOSITE The artist worked over all the areas of the painting at the same time, moving from foreground to background and constantly making small adjustments. The final touches were the fine lines of white to indicate the fold of the curtain on the left, and the addition of a cushion to the chair. This forms a triangle just intersecting the horizontal of the window sill.

MATERIALS USED

- Support: bought canvas board 51 × 40 cm (20 × 16 in)
- Brushes: bristle, number 12 flat and number 6 filbert. Turpentine was used to dilute the paint in the early stages
- Colours: titanium white, vermilion, cadmium red, cobalt violet, raw umber, Indian red, yellow ochre, chrome green, oxide of chromium, ultramarine blue and cerulean blue. (Vermilion is a very expensive colour, but is occasionally necessary for a subject like this, which relies on vivid and pure colours)

6

GERANIUM IN A POT

Some people regard flower painting as a rather limited branch of art, but there is no reason for this attitude, as there are almost as many ways of treating a flower painting as there are of treating a landscape or portrait. Flowers can be painted outdoors as part of a landscape, indoors as part of a still-life, or simply by themselves, like the illustrations to natural-history books. In the previous painting, the flowers were only one element in a busy composition, while here one simple bloom in an undecorated pot forms the whole painting.

The problem with flowers is the same as with still-life – how to make an interesting and well-balanced arrangement that you can translate into paint without getting too bogged down in the minute details. Artists of the past, particularly the Dutch 17th-century masters, tended towards very elaborate arrangements with many different blooms, often in intricate and beautiful porcelain vases, which were really exercises in the minute depiction of fine detail, but this painting demonstrates how a simple subject can make an exciting painting.

As can be seen from the photograph, the artist has considerably exaggerated the angle of the flower head and the length of the stalk in order to give a diagonal emphasis to the subject, and has strengthened this by means of the slightly curving diagonal lines in the background and on the slanting edge of the skirting board. Placing the pot below eye-level has allowed the rim to be shown as a definite curve and the shadow to assume importance as part of the composition. The result is simple but pleasing; like most good paintings, this one looks deceptively easy.

The paint here has been used thickly, unlike that in the previous painting. Parts of the background were applied with a palette knife, with the side of the knife used to make sharply defined lines on the leaves. The flower heads were built up in thick impasto; in some places the brushstrokes themselves form the petals and in other places paint has been squeezed on direct from the tube, so that the painting has an interesting and varied surface. This is particularly important in a subject as stark as this, which might have looked rather dull and lifeless. A good artist plans the paint surface as carefully as the composition, so that it forms an integral part of the whole, rather than just letting it happen, but accidental effects can often be used to advantage also, and can frequently give rise to a new technique that can be put to use in a subsequent painting.

1

ABOVE **1** A few lines made with a sharp pencil served to place the main shapes, which were then quickly blocked in with bright colours. Even at this stage the paint was used quite thickly, as can be seen on the flower pot and the leaves at the top.

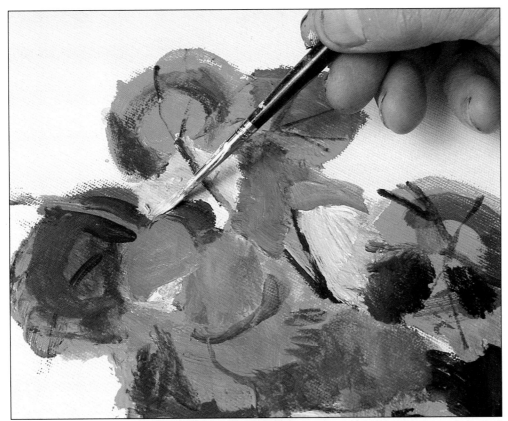

3

LEFT **2** AND ABOVE **3** The
diagonal line for the edge of
the skirting board was
painted in next, together
with an area of colour around
the pot (ABOVE), acting as a
key for the other colours. The
photograph (LEFT) shows
thick white paint being
applied with a small brush to
sharpen and define the edges
of the leaves and stems.

LEFT **4** Here a medium-sized
round brush is being used to
apply thick paint to the
flower heads so that the
brushstrokes themselves
form the shapes of the petals,
and a special impasto
medium was mixed with the
paint to give it extra body.
This is a good example of
using particular brushes to
create particular effects; a
flat brush would not have
been suitable for this
purpose.

2

4

RIGHT **5** Here the flat of the painting knife has been used to apply thick white paint to an area of the background, giving a lively, rough-textured effect.

5

MATERIALS USED

- Support: canvas board 51 × 40 cm (20 × 16 in)
- Brushes: white bristle numbers 3, 4 and 6 (and a palette knife)
- Colours: titanium white, alizarin crimson, cadmium red, viridian, Prussian blue, raw umber and Payne's grey. The impasto medium, *Oleopasto,* was mixed with the paint in the areas where it was applied thickly

RIGHT **6** This detail shows the way the paint has been built up quite thickly on the highlight areas of the leaves so that they stand out from the areas of thinner, darker paint. The lines of dark green radiating from the centres of the leaves were made with the edge of a painting knife.

OPPOSITE The final touches involved more work on the background, foreground and shadow areas, so that the background is now perceived as an uneven piece of white fabric with folds and creases. There is just enough texture and detail to give interest to the painting without in any way detracting from the plant itself. The floor in front of the pot, previously painted flat, has now been broken up with short, stabbing brushstrokes, indicating an uneven fall of light.

6

INTERIOR WITH BROOM

THIS kind of painting, of familiar objects in a domestic setting, has always been popular with artists, and has its roots in the lovely, tranquil interiors of the Dutch painters of the 17th century. Probably the most famous of all such paintings in more modern times is Van Gogh's *Yellow Chair,* but the French artists Edouard Vuillard (1868-1940) and Pierre Bonnard (1867-1947), among others, also painted many exquisite interiors. Looking at such paintings, one often has the feeling that the artists were fortunate in having rooms that look so much more attractive than our own. This is, of course, sometimes well justified, since few people live in houses with fine views or with large shuttered windows, but this painting demonstrates what can be done with seemingly quite unpromising material – just a corner with a broom and a hat hanging on the wall. The artist has aimed at creating a feeling of quiet domestic intimacy by the choice of a subject in which there is no drama and no main focal point.

Here the artist had a very clear vision of how the painting was to look, and went about organizing it with this vision in mind. It is basically abstract in feeling, with no bright colours; so only a small palette was used. The main lines are vertical, with the diagonals at the bottom of the wall and door forming a zigzag line from left to right. What the artist had to consider was the balance of the lines and shapes and that of the lights and darks, all of which were planned with great care. Any change in the composition – for example, reducing the width of the door, removing the hat, or making the area of black floor larger – would upset the balance quite seriously.

Because the subject is such a stark and goemetric one, the artist has chosen to use his paint fairly thinly, to emphasize these qualities, and has created small areas of texture by drawing with a pencil and spattering the paint in places. He has also used masking tape to ensure that the vertical and diagonal lines are really straight and true, with clean, hard edges. In a painting like this, any deviation from a true parallel, however small, would completely destroy the effect.

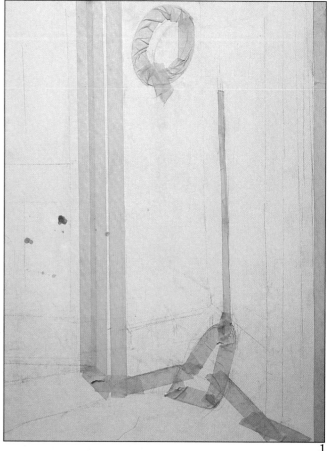

1

ABOVE **1** The first step was to make a very careful drawing, using a sharp pencil, a ruler and a set square. Masking tape was then placed over all the edges, so that the preliminary stage of this painting looks quite unlike the more conventional drawing or underpainting.

LEFT **2** AND OPPOSITE TOP LEFT **3** Paint was applied quite freely over the masking tape with a medium-sized flat bristle brush.

2

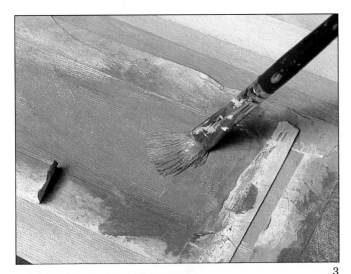

ABOVE **4** As soon as the tape was dry it was lifted, giving sharp, clean edges. Care must be taken when using this technique not to use the paint too thinly or it will seep under the tape.

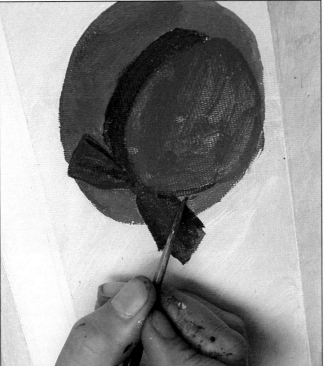

ABOVE **5** The large area of the walls was covered with quite thick paint, a mixture of titanium white modified with small quantities of Payne's grey, raw sienna and cobalt blue.

LEFT **6** The underpainting was now complete, and the paint sufficiently dry to work on. Here the artist is using a small sable brush to paint small details of the hat and ribbon.

FAR LEFT **7** By this stage all the canvas had been covered and the main areas were more or less complete, but the focus of interest, the broom, needed further definition and texture.

LEFT **8** The artist re-tapes the edges of the broom and places newspaper over the rest of the painting to protect it, leaving exposed the small area of skirting board around the broom. He then loads a bristle brush with thinned paint and spatters it with his finger.

7

8

MATERIALS USED

- Support: fine-grained canvas board 51 × 40 cm (20 × 16 in) (a surface particularly well-suited to this type of 'hard-edge' painting)
- Brushes: medium-sized flat bristle and a number 6 sable
- Colours: titanium white, Payne's grey, raw sienna, burnt umber, cobalt blue, viridian and cadmium red

9

10

ABOVE LEFT **9** AND ABOVE RIGHT **10** The bristles of the broom are suggested by firstly drawing into the thin, dry paint with a pencil and then by scratching the paint away with the handle of a brush.

OPPOSITE A comparison of the finished painting with the earlier stage clearly shows how important the final touches were. The eye is now drawn to the textured broom and spattered area of skirting board, whereas

previously the painting had rather the appearance of a stage set waiting for something to happen, without a 'focal point'. The colours are muted, the atmosphere is calm.

GLOSSARY

ABSTRACT Relying on colour, pattern and form rather than the realistic or naturalistic portrayal of subject matter.

ABSTRACTION The creation of an abstract image by the simplification of natural appearances.

ADVANCING COLOURS Colours which appear to be near the viewer. Warm, strong colours seem to advance whereas cool colours recede.

AERIAL PERSPECTIVE The use of colour and tone to indicate space and recession. Warm colours, clearly defined forms and sharp contrasts of tone tend to advance towards the picture plane whereas cool colours, less clearly defined forms and tonal contrasts appear farther away.

ALLA PRIMA Direct painting in which the picture is completed in one session without any underpainting or underdrawing.

BINDER A liquid medium which is mixed with powdered pigment to form a paint. Linseed oil is the most common binding medium for oil paint, although poppy and safflower oils are sometimes used for paler colours. The binding medium oxidizes to form a skin in which the pigments are held in suspension.

BLENDING Merging adjacent colour areas so that the transition between the colours is imperceptible.

BLOCKING IN The first stage of a painting in which the main forms of the composition are laid down in approximate areas of tone and colour.

BROKEN COLOUR A term used in colour theory to describe a colour mixed from two secondary colours. These colours tend towards grey. It is also a method of painting in which colours are applied as areas of pure paint rather than being blended or mixed. These colours combine in the eye of the viewer to create new colours. The paint may be applied in small discrete patches, as in the Pointillist technique, or it may be applied in such a way that initial paint layers show through subsequent layers to create new colours.

CHIAROSCURO The exploitation of light and shadow within a painting. The term is usually applied to the work of painters such as Rembrandt and Caravaggio whose paintings are predominantly dark in tone.

COMPLEMENTARY COLOURS The colours that appear at opposite sides of the colour wheel. Complementary pairs include orange and blue, yellow and violet and red and green. Complementary colours placed side by side tend to enhance each other, thus red placed alongside a complementary green

appears richer than if it stands on its own.

COMPOSITION The organization of colour and form within a picture area.

COVERING POWER This term refers to the opacity or transparency of a paint. Some paints are transparent and are therefore more suitable for glazing whereas opaque paints are used for areas of dense colour or where it is important to obliterate underlying colour.

DILUENT A liquid such as turpentine which is used to dilute paint. It evaporates completely and has no binding effect on the pigment.

DRY BRUSH In this technique dry paint is dragged across the surface of a painting, so that it adheres to the raised areas, creating broken areas of colour.

FERRULE The metal collar of a brush which secures the bristles to the handle.

FIGURATIVE ART Also known as representational art, it depicts recognizable objects such as the human figure.

FUGITIVE This term describes pigments which fade on exposure to light.

GLAZING The application of a transparent film of colour over a lighter, opaque colour. It is sometimes used to modify darker colours.

GROUND A ground or priming is a surface which has been specially prepared to accept oil paint. The ground serves two purposes: it isolates the support from the paint and it provides the painter with a pleasant surface to paint on.

HUE This term indicates the type of colour in terms of its blueness, redness or yellowness. About 150 different hues can be recognized.

IMPASTO Paint applied thickly so that it retains the mark of the brush or the knife. Initially impasto was used only in small areas of the painting by painters such as Titian and Rembrandt. Later, painters like Van Gogh exploited the expressive possibilities of impasto, applying paint 'alla prima' using a loaded brush or knife.

LEAN A term used to describe oil paint which has little or no added oil. The expression 'fat over lean' refers to the use of lean paint (thinned with turpentine or white spirit) under paint layers into which more oil is progressively introduced. This method of working prevents the paint surface from cracking as it dries.

LINEAR PERSPECTIVE A method of creating an illusion of depth and three dimensions on a flat surface through the use of converging lines and vanishing points.

LOCAL COLOUR The actual colour of the surface of an

object unmodified by light, shade or distance.

MAHL STICK A cane used for steadying the painting arm when putting in fine detail. One end is covered with a soft pad to prevent the point from damaging the support.

MASK Tape or paper used to isolate a particular area of a painting. This allows the artist to work freely in the rest of the painting. Masks can also be used to create special edges and shapes. Frame-shaped masks or masks made from two L-shaped pieces of paper or card can be used as an aid to composition. They are placed on a sketch or preparatory study so that the artist can select the area of the image to be used and the shape of the final painting.

MEDIUM The material used for painting or drawing, such as water-colour, pencil or oil paint. The term is also used to describe a binding substance which is added to pigment to make paint; for example, the binding medium for watercolour is gum arabic and for oil paint it is linseed oil. The third meaning of the word describes substances which are added to paint while painting or drawing to modify the way in which the paint behaves. These may be traditional mediums like poppy oil, copal oil or a varnish, or they may be commercial mediums such as Win-gel, Oleopasto or Liquin.

MODELLING The three-dimensionality of objects in painting or drawings, suggested by various methods including the variation of tones.

MONOCHROME A painting executed in black and white, or black, white and one other colour.

NEGATIVE SPACE The spaces between and around the main elements of the subject – the background in a figure painting, for example.

OPACITY The ability of a pigment to cover and obscure the surface or colour to which it is applied.

OPTICAL COLOUR MIXING Creating new colours by mixing pigments optically on the canvas rather than on the palette. The Pointillists placed small dots of unmixed colour on the canvas so that viewed from a distance the dots are no longer visible and, for example, dabs of yellow and red would combine in the eye of the viewer to create orange.

PAINTING KNIFE A knife with a thin flexible blade used for applying paint to a support. These knives generally have a cranked handle and are available in a range of shapes and sizes.

PALETTE KNIFE A knife with a straight steel blade used for mixing paint on the palette, cleaning the palette and for scraping paint from the support if necessary.

PICTURE PLANE The imaginary vertical plane which separates the viewer's world from that of the picture. The surface of the picture.

PLANES The flat surfaces of an object. These are revealed by light and can be seen in terms of light and dark. Even a curved surface can be regarded as an infin ite number of small planes.

PLEIN AIR A French term meaning 'open air' used to describe pictures painted out of doors.

PRIMARY COLOURS These are colours which cannot be obtained by mixing other colours. The paint primaries are red, yellow and blue.

PRIMING Also known as ground, this is the layer or layers of materials applied to a support to make it less absorbent or more pleasant to paint on. A suitable priming for canvas could consist of a layer of size, followed by an oil ground.

RENAISSANCE The cultural revival of classic ideals which took place in Europe from the fourteenth to the sixteenth centuries.

SATURATED COLOUR Pure colour, free of black and white and therefore intense.

SCUMBLING Dryish, opaque paint which is brushed freely over preceding layers so that the underlying colour, or the support, shows through in places.

SIZE Gelatinous solution, such as rabbitskin glue, which is used to seal the support.

STAINING POWER The colouring strength of a pigment and its ability to impart that colour to white, or to a mixture. If a pigment has good staining power you will need only a little of it to impart colour to a mixture.

STIPPLE The use of dots in painting, drawing or engraving, instead of line or flat colour.

SUPPORT A surface for painting or drawing, which could be canvas, board or paper.

TONE The degree of lightness or darkness. The tone of a colour is assessed independently of its hue.

UNDERDRAWING The preliminary drawing for a painting, often done in pencil, charcoal or paint.

UNDERPAINTING The preliminary blocking-in of the main forms, colours and tonal areas.

WASH An application of thinly diluted paint.

WET INTO DRY The application of paint to a completely dry surface.

wet in wet The application of wet paint to an already wet surface. Used in the alla prima technique. Wet in wet allows the artist to blend colours and tones.

INDEX